CW01467273

To: Jo & Andy.

The Griffith Years

Regards!
Mike Mooney
10/03

the Griffith Years

History of the Griffith Motorcar, 1963 – 1967... and beyond

by

Mike Mooney

Copyright 2003 Mike Mooney

www.griffithyears.com

ISBN 0-9741307-0-2

Written and designed by Mike Mooney

Cover Art by Gerry Mooney

www.mooneyart.com

WE'RE PROUD TO PRESENT
the Grrrrreat GRIFFITH Series 200

... world's fastest, most dramatic, most economical production automobile. With a standard 289 cubic inch, 195 horsepower Ford V-8 engine, the GRIFFITH Series 200 is truly the car that goes like all get-out, for those who like to get out and GO!

SPECIFICATIONS

ENGINE

Type	Ford V-8
Displacement	289 cu. in. (4727 cc)
Valve Position	Overhead
Bore	4.00 in.
Stroke	2.87 in.
Max. B.H.P.	195 @ 4400 RPM (Std.)
Clutch	10½ in. dia. hydraulic
Gearbox	Ford—all synchromesh, 4-speeds and reverse

CHASSIS

Frame	Multi-tubular
Suspension	Independent all-round coil springs with unequal length wishbones
Brakes	Front, Girling 10¾" discs Rear, Girling drums 9"x1¾"
Dampers	Woodhead-Monroe telescopic hydraulic
Wheels	Knock-off, 72 spoke wire wheels
Tires	Dunlop SP 185x15
Steering	Rack and pinion

BODY

Construction	Reinforced fiberglas on multitubular frame— insulated for sound deadening
Doors	Two doors with roll-up windows
Seating	Two competition type bucket seats upholstered in high grade leather grain vinyl
Steering Wheel	15" dia., 3 spoke, wood rim competition type
Instruments	Separate rev. counter, trip speedometer, oil pressure, water temperature, ammeter and fuel gage
Fuel Tank	16 gal. (U.S.) located in rear with quick release filler

DIMENSIONS

Wheelbase	85½ in.
Track	Front 52½ in. Rear 54 in.
Over-all Length	138 in.
Over-all Height	48 in.
Over-all Width	64 in.
Ground Clearance	6 in.
Curb Weight	1450 pounds dry

GRIFFITH FACTORY INSTALLED OPTIONS

Ford V-8 289 cu. in., 271 B.H.P., high-performance engine	$495.00
Fresh Air Heater & Defroster	$ 62.00
Regulation Seat Belts (both seats)	$ 14.00
Luggage Rack (chrome)	$ 37.00
Competition Vehicles & Related Racing & Performance Equipment	(Prices available on request)

The Griffith Series 200 is available in the following range of Standard Colors:

British Racing Green	*Cirrus White
Signal Red	Regal Red * Black
Silver Blue	Powder Blue

Interiors:

*Cherry Red   Finnish Black

Prices and Specifications Subject to Change without Notice.

WE'RE PROUD TO PRESENT
the Grrrrreat GRIFFITH Series 400

271 HP High Performance Ford 289 cu. in. engine; Fully Synchronized close ratio 4 speed manual transmission; Full instrumentation; Electric windshield wipers; Self-cancelling directional indicators; Heater; Seat belts; Rack & Pinion steering; All New handling package; Wood rim steering wheel; 72-spoke Dunlop knock-off wire wheels and SP 185x15 Dunlop tires; Disc brakes front and drum brakes rear; Front anti-roll bar. Adjustable seats; Padded sun visors; Adjustable interior mirror; Padded dash; Reversing lamps; Center horn button; Salisbury Rear; 160 MPH Speedometer; 8000 R.P.M. Tachometer.

SPECIFICATIONS

ENGINE

Ford	V8
Displacement	289 cu. in. (4727cc)
Valve Position	Overhead
Bore	4.00 in.
Stroke	2.87 in.
Compression Ratio	10.1
BPH @ RPM	271-6000
Torque at RPM	312-3400
Carburetor	Carter 4 Barrel
Fuel required	Premium Grade
Clutch Type	Single Plate Dry dia. 10½

TRANSMISSION

No. Gears	Forward 4
	Reverse 1
All Synchro and close ratio	

BODY

Construction	Reinforced fiberglas on multitubular frame —insulated for sound deadening
Doors	2 with roll-up windows
Seats	2 Bucket Type
Upholstery	Leather grained vinyl
Steering Wheel	15″ dia. 3 spoke, wood rim competition type

CHASSIS

Multi Tubular	Frame
Suspension	Independent 4 – wheel
Number Shocks	2 front
	4 rear
Brakes	Girling
Front	Discs 10¾ in.
Rear	Drum 9x1.75
Dampers	Woodhead-Monroe Telescopic Hydraulic
Steering	Rack & Pinion

DIMENSIONS

Wheelbase	85½ in.
Track	Front 52½
	Rear 54 in.
Over-all Length	138 in.
Over-all Height	48 in.
Over-all Width	64 in.
Ground Clearance	6 in.
Curb Weight	1850 pounds dry

Griffith Series 400 cars are available in the following colors:

Signal Red	Regal Red
Cirrus White	British Racing Green
Silver Blue	Powder Blue

Prices and Specifications Subject to Change without Notice.

Wouldn't you expect a lot from a car that looked like this?

17 facts you should know about the new Griffith sports car. The 18th is that parts for it are in stock in more than 4000 U.S. cities and towns.

1. Styling that can only be described as *taut*. No embellishment of any kind. From any quarter it looks small, almost feline, in its grace. Very fast, very Italian. *Bellissima!*

2. The Griffith styling is practical. The doors are large, giving easy entrance and exit. (But duck your head, it is *low*.) More than enough room for luggage for the two of you (and *wide* enough for golf bags!). The frontal area is extremely small, and the shape is wind-cheating, combining to boost gas mileage.

3. The Griffith body is all steel, welded into a single rattle-free unit. Because it is steel, wherever you go the local body and 'fender man can take out your dinks. No specialized equipment or techniques required.

4. You are cradled in a seat that wraps around your hips and holds you firmly in position . . . a driving throne. Great care has been taken to position all controls so they come immediately to hand. And you can *see* all four corners.

5. The carpeted interior is finished in softly tough vinyl by fine old Italian hands, *con amore*. (Elegant Onyx or Palomino leather is optional at added cost.) The instruments are shaded to keep reflections out of the windshield. All the necessary instruments are there, big and round, with white letters on black dials . . . good-looking, good looking at.

6. The Griffith is built to exceptional standards . . . mostly by hand.

And it goes like the clappers . . .

7. Up front a big Plymouth Commando 273 cu. in. engine. Comfortably, with room to get at it. With a couple million Plymouths on the roads, you know parts are in stock almost anywhere. (And rafts of hop-up equipment too.)

8. How do you like your power delivered—four-on-the-floor or automatic? Both are standard Plymouth items. (*Their* advertising will tell you how trouble-free these transmissions are.)

9. Okay, so it goes like the clappers—how does it stop? 10-inch disc brakes on *all four* wheels pull you down from *any* speed in half the distance of ordinary drums. Wet or dry. Squarely and surely. Time after time after time after time . . .

10. While the rear axle is also a standard item, we mount it differently. Trailing links on each side and a Panhard rod keep the axle in its place, eliminating wind up and wheel hop. More satisfactory than all but the most complicated independent rear suspensions . . . and utterly reliable.

11. With a weight of only 2540 pounds, you might expect we would worry about delivering 235 horsepower to the road. We did. The answer is partly in the suspension (thanks to assistance from John Crosthwaite of BRM, the British Grand Prix champions) and partly in the wide-based wheels and big Goodyear Red Line nylon tires. They lay down a big footprint, quietly, smoothly.

The best handling you've had since you were a baby . . .

12. If it looks good, and goes good, how do you make it handle? Having a knowledgeable person lay out the suspension (one with Gran Prix experience) was the start. Then, have a successful racing driver/engineer tune it. (Our Chief Engineer finished third in the Daytona 24-hour.) Results:

13. The Griffith goes precisely where you steer it . . . to a quarter of an inch . . . with its rack and pinion steering. The steering wheel (wood rimmed on spring steel) goes 3 turns lock-to-lock so that you rarely have to lift your hands from the wheel. Just when parking.

14. Even though the engine is in front, weight is shaded aft . . . 53% on the rear wheels. A slight understeer under all conditions means that the Griffith is steady, never "quick." Goes around corners like a cat on a carpet.

15. You don't *have* to be a highly skilled race driver to enjoy the Griffith. But we dare say you will want to drive with the precision of a professional.

For prospective Griffith owners only . . .

16. . . . take note: We expect to build 512 cars this year. By hand, remember? There are both a coupe and a convertible. There are about a dozen colors available. Heater is standard, as are most of the usual options. The 7-transistor radio is optional.

17. At $6,095 the demand is enthusiastic, con *brio*. But the supply is *moderato*. See one of our dealers about reserving a production line position, and take a look at our colorful 8-page brochure. Or write for your copy (with 25¢ to cover handling) to Mr. A. J. "Jack" Griffith, Griffith Motors, Inc., 1478 Old Country Road, Plainview, N.Y. 11803.

GRIFFITH
Plymouth Powered

the Griffith Years

History of the Griffith motorcar
1963 – 1967 and beyond

By

Mike Mooney

Possum Valley Publishers   Post Office Box 1117   Claremont, North Carolina 28610

The Griffith Years

Contents

The Griffith Years

Acknowledgments

In early 1990 when I formed the basic ideas to take the loose threads and make a finely stitched quilt of the Griffith motorcar history I had one strong friend whose incessant ramblings kept the fire alive.

Bill "Willie" Seitz seemed to have a bullet-proof, almost perfect recall of names and events not only of the Griffith years but also of the early and exciting days of hot rods and race cars on Long Island.

Being an early student of Willie, I hung around this guy, some say too long. Willie, who could have easily been lumped into the description of an "eccentric," was interesting enough for me to hang around just one day longer because I only wanted to see what would happen next. Those extra hours spent with Willie coupled with my access to a neat computer and an inbred curiosity for "just the facts" paid off when I started the interviews.

Then came the search for the people who I kept in my memories of the Griffith automobile and I started to make notes. With notes about the specific and the arcane, asking questions wherever I traveled, I went looking for that next piece of information.

Jack Griffith and his lovely wife, Marge, were first on my list of visits and he must have wondered whether this would fly. Jack and I had met a few times since that first stop and on each visit the conversations widened as old memories were rekindled.

Now that the horse was out of the barn I started the task of calling on many of the people who were part of the mosaic. Joe Quinn, the salesman who sold me the Mustang back in '64 and I were constants and we chatted. Joey Detore, part of the story, was gone now, a victim of Lou Gehrig's disease.

Pete Elardo, a salesman at White-Griffith Ford would go on to become the sales manager at another Ford dealership, helped with a few anecdotes, but he, too, left us too early.

The Griffith Years

Dave Schineller and John Fisher were my next contacts and they weren't too sure that they could add much to the mix but, as time would prove, the puzzle had too many blanks and they each had some pieces to add.

Then a call came in from Walter Armstrong in Maine telling me that he had located the elusive Lew Schulz. He was in Maine and wanted to meet with me for an interview. We made two interviews with Lew, the other in New Jersey and recorded them both on videotape. The only down side to that meeting was that a short time later while I was on the road doing some other interviews, my truck was vandalized in Columbus, Ohio and the camera with the stills of Lew was gone… the videos were safe. I learned a hard lesson from that incident.

Then one day I had the opportunity to be researching a story on a '63 Z-06 Corvette and during the interview I naturally brought up the subject of the Griffith. The car owner was familiar with the car and asked if I had seen Len Bailey lately. I had lost track but it turned out that Len was just a scant few miles from my home base and we hooked up for lunch. The engine was revving!

The Jefferson 500, a vintage race at Summit Point, brought several Griffiths and Jack himself together for an historic meeting. The word was spreading and stories, some believable, many not, were surfacing.

A hiatus to build a new home in North Carolina yielded yet another contact for me. Larry Jenkins, a former Holman-Moody employee who was in charge of the Omega project, was located just a few miles outside of Charlotte and we chatted more than once.

Steve Wilder, a friend who was involved with the post-Griffith automobile sales, sat down for an interview inside a noisy, midtown New York diner and was most helpful.

Random information sifted through the cracks and the project continued. I got a call that Gerry Sagerman could be contacted in Florida. We met and another interview was a wrap. Gerry and Delores were perfect hosts for the visit, and again, Willie was there with me.

Hayes Harris, who will probably go down in automotive history as the "Griffith Salesman of the Century," got my ear and we met at his shop in Vero Beach where, not one, but three Griffiths were for sale in the showroom. Again, the pieces were falling together.

The Griffith Years

The stage was about to be set for one of the greatest meetings in Griffith lore. At the annual Greenwich (Conn.) Concours d'Elegance I met with a fellow judge, Joe Dockery, who said that he could help me find George Clark. We made the contact and then more doors were opened.

With a great deal of assistance from Frank Gardner, the executive director of the Saratoga Automobile Museum in Saratoga Springs, New York I seated several members of the original Griffith Team together for a group-videotaped interview on August 10, 2002.

Len Bailey, Karen Bocsusis, George Clark, John Fisher, Dave Schineller, Willie Seitz and Roger Teck met for the first time in more than 33 years and the group was collected around a beautiful Griffith Series 200 owned by Russ Rogers who brought the car in for the day.

An interesting sideline was that my production assistant for the day was Willie and Joyce Seitz's grandson, Ryan Brophy. The beat goes on.

When it came to researching the TVR part of the book, the one source who was always "on call" was the current president of the TVR Car Club of North America (TVRCCNA), Marshall Moore. We had many hours of calls clearing up some of the gray area that existed in the historical catacombs of Hoo Hill.

There were also times that I had to get an arcane bit of current knowledge regarding the Griffith archives and Joe Rauh always came through in a pinch. As president of the Griffith Car Club, he opened the books to us when we needed some updates on ownership and history of some of the cars. Joe also took the time to visit Willie and me on a cross country business trip. I think I owe him a steak dinner for that one.

Lastly, I want to recognize my wife, Ellen. Often lost in the trivia that I reveled in as well as the many calls at odd hours that kept me busy well into the early morning, Ellen had no idea what was in the offing but she believed in my quest. This wonderful, retired English teacher was also my proof reader and grammar coach. Thanks coach!

Mike Mooney

𝔉𝔬𝔯𝔢𝔴𝔬𝔯𝔡

J ack Griffith did two things in his life which allowed this writer to accomplish a few of his often-scattered goals. His first was to hire an automobile salesman who sold me a foolishly-fast car and the second was to give this writer free rein to present you with the story of one of Jack's dreams... The Griffith Motorcar.

Early in 1964 the news was leaking from some very porous containers that Ford Motor Company (Ford) was on the verge of introducing a new car from its stable. In April of that year, the Mustang trotted into the corporate corral and would set the stage for the Pony Car revolution. One month later I was lured to a showroom on Long Island looking for a young and energetic salesman named Joe Quinn who said that I could own one of these neat cars for a mere ten percent over dealer cost.

Joe worked at Griffith Ford in Hicksville, Long Island, New York and on June 22, 1964, after setting the ground rules for the game I quickly ordered a '65 Mustang with the Vehicle Identification Number of 5F07K293364, a fabled Cobra powered HiPo (high performance) 289 cubic inch displacement, 271 horsepower muscle car that was to sate my need for speed.

In my former lifetime spent somewhat errantly as a police officer on the Suffolk County, NY, Police Department, one of my assignments was as a Highway Patrol officer pacing the infamous Long Island Expressway (L.I.E.). One evening I happened upon a disabled motorist who had run out of gas. The car was a strange-looking shave-tail which I recognized as a Griffith and the driver was very familiar. There, on the side of this busy highway, sat an embarrassed Mark Donohue in a Griffith with the fuel gauge on "E."

During the round trip to the Sunoco gas station on Rt. 110 in Melville, Mark was curious about my involvement with the sporty car, club racing crowd and my need for speed. By the time we got the Ford engine fired up in this little fiberglass car he had invited me back to his office in the morning for a meeting.

The Griffith Years

The following day at the Griffith Motorcar corporate offices I learned that Mark had a dire need for someone who knew how to handle a fast car and to provide him with a good "seat-of-the-pants" evaluation of this strange car.

Secondly, since they didn't have corporate funding for an official test track, previous drivers had to use the L.I.E. and often returned with a traffic summons or two. Mark said he needed someone of "my professional stature" to preclude any further traffic court visits. The only caveat was that this was an unsalaried position but the "perks" were great. They included a test car to drive around whenever I wanted and that I could "pit" for him whenever I was available. I signed on immediately!

Because of these two somewhat unrelated situations, Andrew J. "Jack" Griffith was totally responsible for these words to eventually be put into print for you all to read.

By the way, as you read through these pages, you might notice that some of the photographs appear to be a bit "seedy" or of a lower content quality than you are used to seeing in print, but since the Griffith records were most likely lost to the dust bin a long time ago we had to rely on several sources who were lucky enough to have saved some of those historical shots.

Enjoy reading *The Griffith Years*.

Mike Mooney

About the cover car

Editor's note: Gracing the cover of this book is a beautiful Series 200, #153. It's owned by Russ Rogers who has been very helpful whenever we needed a car to show for presentation to the media or just to have fun. I thought that we would give Russ this space to present his own story to the readers.

By Russ Rogers

One lazy, warm spring evening in 1966, I had been quaffing a few cool ones with some friends in a tavern in Bronxville, New York just north of the big city, having some fun and talking about just about everything that we were all interested in, including cars. As we were leaving, I spotted this very wild looking silver car parked across the street. It caught my eye because it was different, very different, from any car I had ever seen.

It was small, really small and the back was quite abbreviated, like it was cut off with a cleaver. The car was also very low to the ground and sat on grey painted wire wheels with knock offs. It had vents, louvers and a big wide mouth opening where the grill should be, that was stuffed with two fans sitting in front of the radiator. There was a bulge in the middle of the hood, a set of dual exhausts in the rear, an emblem that said "Powered by Ford" and a badge that said "Griffith"

Holy moly. There it sat in all its nastiness, looking like it was ready to explode down the road. I kept walking around, checking it out and just shaking my head. Truly a mean looking car, especially when you know what killer performance it is capable of. I never forgot my first encounter. For twenty years, that was the only time I would see a Griffith on the street; a very rare car indeed.

 Fast forward to late fall, 1986, and with the elusive Griffith always in the back of my mind, a friend brings me an ad for a 1965 Series 200 for sale. A phone call to the owner, and we were off, to examine a legend close up. The car was in Scarsdale, about fifteen minutes from my home. As we were being led into the garage, I can remember my anticipation level was rising up to almost uncontrollable.

Then, there it was. Off the road since 1969, sat a very original Griffith. Totally amazed, I asked questions like "Is it a HiPo?" and "Is this an original?" The answers were yes and yes. Everything was there. Nothing was missing, which after twenty years, was a find because all kinds of things usually get lost or thrown away.

The car appeared to be in a light grey primer, but the owner said that when he purchased the car, in 1966 from the original owner, the car had already been repaint silver

16

over the factory red and that the silver had faded to a dull grey. Hearing that, I related the story to him about the Bronxville car to which he replied, "I used to live in Bronxville." Twenty years of stun must have crossed my face. Here I am looking at the same, one and only Griffith that I had seen back in 1966. Unbelievable! We talked some more and after a very interesting hour, we left, but for me, this was going to be just the beginning.

For days, all I could think about was that silver car. I had to have it. You know how that goes. So, now began the task of trying to convince my wife that we needed another car/project and that we could afford to buy it. Well, as it turned out, I didn't have to wait very long. About two weeks later, my wife had struck a deal, through my friend, with the owner of the Griffith. I left work one day to find an early Christmas present sitting in the parking lot. I owned a Griffith!

Many enjoyable years have passed and 200-5-153 has been repainted and gone through mechanically to make it safer and more street worthy (and a little bit quicker!) Driving it is always a treat. Pick a gear, any gear. Around town it can be driven in just one gear, almost like an automatic. 35 mph in 1st is no problem with the 3:54 gears that put the 1-2 up shift at around 90 mph at 7000 rpm. 15 mph in 4th is also comfy because, with just five-pound per horsepower, you just touch the gas and go. No lugging, just "goodbye!"

First gear just gets you started and you settle in to where you are going and how fast you are getting there. If you punch it at 5 mph, it won't even chirp. Just sheer forward motion. Kind of like a motorcycle, light weight, and all that. Second pulls like a locomotive.

Third is not for the faint of heart, if in fact, you've made it this far. This is a gear that requires lots of nerve because you are accelerating at almost the same rate as the lower gears but you are covering major ground. Hundreds of feet of it a second. By this point, most passengers are either frozen stiff or squirming in their seat and making nervous small talk. Some just scream. Fourth, well fourth is a pure religious experience.

After you've done the little 8 or 10 second exercise above, you can then settle into some extremely enjoyable, twisty country road and drive the car like it was meant to be driven. Up, down, around, point and shoot, back off, great motor and exhaust sounds. The most effortless sports car I have ever driven. Light, quick and comfortable and just plain fun!

Thank you, Jack Griffith.

ALL ABOUT THIS 1965 GRIFFITH 200-5-153

Body

Manufacturer - Griffith Motors
Body Material - Fiberglass
Weight - 1980 lbs. w/full fuel
Body - weight 125 lbs.
Wheelbase - 85.5
Length - 138
Ground Clearance - Scrapes on almost everything
Paint - Glasurit
Seats - Original
Seat Belts - R.J.S. 5 point harness with quick release
Carpet - Wilton wool
Steering Wheel - Original wood over aluminum 3 spoke
Rear View Mirror - Original Barnacle
Headlights - Original Lucas
Taillights - Original Sparto
Rear Window - Ferron Plexiglas
Roll Bar - Ferron custom

Drive Train

Engine - Original Ford 289 HIPO, balanced and blueprinted
Horsepower - 350+/-
Horsepower to Weight ratio – approx. 5.65 lbs. per hp
Cam - Crane
Ignition - Crane
Wiring - Original Lucas for the most part
Valves - Triple cut
Rockers - Crane roller
Carburetor - Barry Grant stage III, flowed/blueprinted
Headers - Island Racing Service, ceramic coated inside/outside
Exhaust - Island Racing Service with x over, ceramic coated inside/outside
Muffler - Island Racing Service, ceramic coated inside/outside
Transmission - 4 speed aluminum T-10 close ratio 2.20 1st gear
Shifter - Stock
Clutch - Centerforce
Differential - B&M built Jaguar 3.54 limited slip
Rear - Ferron heavy duty half shafts and axles
Chassis - Frame Factory braised tube
Radiator - Cross flow re-cored, original tank, Shelby aluminum overflow tank
Fans - Dual electric Kenlow original
Fuel tank - 8 gal. ATL fuel cell
Fuel Pump - (2) Electric with flip switch
Brakes - Disk front, Drum rear with proportioning valve
Spring/Shocks - front. (2) Alden externally adjustable gas coil-over
Spring/Shocks - rear (4) Spax externally adjustable gas coil-over
Wheels - 72 spoke with knock off
Tires - 195/65 Dunlop Sport

The Griffith Years

The Griffith Years

The Griffith Years

one

Jack

"...A lot of people have dreams of doing things and never do it. I had dreams of what I wanted to do and I did it. I wouldn't change any part of that."

Jack Griffith

J ack Griffith **never** stood still a day in his life. He was born runnin' and hasn't stopped yet. Trying to keep up with Andrew Jackson "Jack" Griffith was a full time job in itself and in his world of business there was no difference.

Growing up in Jackson Heights on the western end of Long Island, Jack was close enough to the big city for the activity that he craved but it was, then, far enough out in the sticks to qualify as country for a young upstart.

Early on, this ardent fan of the Glenn Miller Band had proved that he was headed for something that had an engine, made noise and went fast. North Beach Airport, now named LaGuardia International Airport, near the shores of the Long Island Sound, was a neighborhood fixture. Like any other youngster, Jack yearned to get his driver's license and the aerodrome parking lot was a safe venue to get the necessary practice.

The Griffith Years

Jack's mom, a housewife whose imagination sparked a hobby of writing mystery stories, was also a talented handwriting expert and his dad was employed in the Immigration and Naturalization Service.

At that time of Jack's life, the Vanderbilt family had been using their fifty-mile long private roadway as the site of their annual Vanderbilt Cup races originating in Queens County and finishing at its eastern terminus of Lake Ronkonkoma in Suffolk County. On the international Formula One scene, Tazio Nuvolari was scorching his legendary driving style into the record books.

But rising out of the depths of the Great Depression the nations of the world were affixed to the nasty business of war. The automotive giants had to focus on the war efforts and the assembly lines no longer turned out the nifty and artistic renderings of the Thirties.

But then the war ended and the production lines were again looking to the needs of the civilian population for direction. Emerging from the memories of World War II, Jack Griffith, a twenty-one year old New Yorker, was ready to take on the automotive business world.

One of the business giants of the war was Henry J. Kaiser, an industrial titan who had turned from his wartime ship building empire toward the post-war automobile industry. The odd-looking, yet futuristic Kaiser and Frazer cars looked good to Jack Griffith and he started as a salesman for a Kaiser-Frazer dealership in Glen Cove, Long Island. The cast was being forged.

| Henry J. Kaiser | Joseph Frazer |

Glen Cove was in the Kaiser-Frazer distributor territory of New York City. The original distributor was Regional Motor Sales, 1710 Broadway; in September of 1946, Earl "Madman" Muntz acquired the operation from the factory, and operated it as Muntz Motor Car Company (retail dealership as well as distributor) at the same address until the end of 1947 when he sold the operation back to Kaiser-Frazer Sales Corporation.

Photo courtesy of Kaiser-Fraser Car Club

1949 Frazer Convertible

The factory continued to operate the distributorship as Kaiser-Frazer Sales Corporation until after Kaiser-Frazer acquired the operations of Willys-Overland in early 1953. After that, the K-F operation was phased out, activities moved to the factory-owned Willys facility

Editor's note: Earl Muntz was in the right place (Los Angeles) at the right time (1941). During the war years, he became the biggest used car dealer in the world. By 1947 Earl had continued in his command of the used car market, but had taken on the largest Kaiser-Frazer dealership in the U.S. In 1947 alone he sold $72,000,000 worth of new and used cars. Muntz sold 22,000 new K-F cars that year, which is really impressive when you stop to think, the total K-F output for 1947 was only 147,000. FREDERICK J. ROTH

photo courtesy Frederick J. Roth

1952 Muntz Jet

During his slack time as a car salesman Jack decided to branch out in his interests and after taking a correspondence course in "Sound Engineering" he qualified to work in the professional recording studios in the big city.

The 1948 recording of the vocal by Dusty Fletcher of **"Open The Door, Richard"** was co-engineered by Jack Griffith. This short career was made even shorter when the commuting to New York became too tedious and time-consuming so Jack hung it up for a while to concentrate on cars at the Kaiser-Frazer dealership.

It didn't take too long for the entrepreneurial skills to emerge and Jack and a fellow salesman decided to open a used car lot. The manufacturers couldn't fill the showrooms fast enough and America needed the mobility, even if it was a pre-war clunker.

This idea worked for awhile but something just didn't fit. The partnership dissolved and Jack decided that sound and audio engineering was his calling. Radio station WKBS broadcasting from Oyster Bay, Long Island, NY was looking for a partner and Jack signed on but his heart was still heavily entrenched in the automobile.

An upstart auto manufacturer from upstate Buffalo was looking for distributors to sell its new car dubbed **"The Playboy"** and Jack was interested.

He called on a friend, Bill Odom, a noted airplane pilot, and the two wanted to form a Long Island distributorship but when the car failed to materialize the idea went into the circular file and Jack went back to Kaiser-Frazer for a short time.

photo courtesy Kaiser-Frazer Car Club

1952 Kaiser Sedan

It was 1949 and Jack was anxious to have his own dealership, a showroom and a business that would anchor him to the automotive community as more than a salesman.

Packard Corporation was expanding the line with their "upside-down bathtub" styled cars aimed at the luxury market. In Rockville Centre, a small but wealthy community in Nassau County on the south shore of Long Island, Jack took a chance and bought a Packard franchise. This bedroom community of New York City was ripe for the demographic market that Packard was seeking out and Griffith stuck his toe into the cold, cold waters of seriously selling cars.

The Griffith Years

This worked well and lasted until 1953, an historic benchmark year in the Packard corporate history. The body had gone through a major change and moved into the more flowing lines that marked the opulence of the "chrome age."

After four years in the business Jack thought it was time for a change and sold the dealership that year. He and John White got together with a new dealership and named it White-Griffith Motors DeSoto and Plymouth. Located on Route 106 in Hicksville, the new shop was in a higher growth area and the baby-boomers were buying.

The high performance market was just starting to rev up and the MoPar top dogs weren't going to be left in the dust. High speed cars and larger-than-life engines were rumbling around the streets and hot rodders were talking more and more about this new thing called "high performance."

Ronnie Householder, the head of Chrysler racing was doing his best to build cars for the next generation and in 1955 the doors were flung open. One of these cars, a Plymouth sedan, was prepped and tuned at White-Griffith Motors for a stab at the land speed record that year. It was the first year of the V-8 Plymouth and Ronnie wanted to make it the fastest one on the block.

File photo

1955 Plymouth Belvedere

When it came to choosing a driver, Householder selected Bill Waters a Volkswagen dealer from Manhasset who often drove in stock cars at the old Freeport stadium under the pseudonym of Ted Tappet. When the dust settled at

Daytona they walked away with the class trophy and set the bar a few notches higher for the competition.

A few years earlier, in 1951, Waters was teamed up with Briggs Cunningham at the 24 Hours of LeMans driving the incredible "Le Monstre," Cunningham's wildly unbelievable creation.

As the decade wore on, the cars got faster, the engines got more powerful and the factories were taking note of the "Win On Sunday, Sell On Monday" approach to marketing and Jack Griffith didn't sit still. The DeSoto and Plymouth signs came down and up went the Ford signs.

With John White no longer in the partnership Lou Benny signed on in 1957 and White-Griffith Ford was born. The muscle-car era was well entrenched on the front pages of the motorsports magazines and the manufacturers were moving gobs of cars out America's showrooms.

Every one of the Big Three had their big and powerful engines. Chevrolet had the Power Pack, Chrysler had their 300, Oldsmobile had the Rocket and Ford had the Thunderbird.

Griffith would begin to build the dealership's reputation on the high-performance image that Dearborn was banking on and he decided to do it well. During the late Fifties and early Sixties, often called the "Golden Years" of the high performance automobile industry, "muscle cars" were being introduced on an almost-weekly basis.

Jack Griffith was an automobile entrepreneur and was in love with the high performance aspect of the beast. These factors along with the indomitable spirit of this man would soon blend together to give birth to a new car.

The Griffith Years

two

Genesis

"Knowing Jack Griffith it isn't difficult to imagine what possessed him to transform a mild-mannered little British sports car into a wild, fire-breathing, Mad Max machine. If you ask him today he'd tell you that he'd do it again in a heartbeat."
Mike Mooney

TVR automobiles were not the most ubiquitous of British sports cars populating the American highways in 1963. This fiberglass lightweight was being sold at a few sparse, multi-marqued dealerships and all due to one, somewhat, inspired racing buff.

Trevor Wilkinson, the father of TVR (name formed by taking three letters from his name), was born in Blackpool, England, in 1923. After leaving school at the age of 14, he began his early life in the automotive field as an apprentice mechanic at the Excel Motor Company, a local garage.

As the wreckage of World War II left its smoldering ruins for the British to repair, Trevor took on the task of setting up his own business, Trevcar Motors in a building that once housed a wheelwright's workshop. The year was 1947.

The Griffith Years

Wilkinson's first attempt at building a "special" car consisted of the marriage between an engine and chassis from an old Alvis Firebird encased in an aluminum body. A very trusting and enthusiastic friend bought it and the company began its historical trip through automotive history.

Jack Pickard joined with Trevor later that year and TVR Engineering was formed, both deciding to build their specials from scratch. Home-building "sports cars" from the ground up was quite common in post-war England.

The first TVR came off the production line two years later with a tubular steel space frame chassis on which panel-beater, Les Dale, hammered out and formed the body panels on the famous English Wheel. The car was equipped and designed with a trailing arm and coil spring suspension and was powered by the ever-faithful "Ford Ten" side-valve engine.

This was followed up by a second car which was custom built for a customer who needed a home for his 1172cc Ford engine.

Fast forward through the next seven years while TVR produced several variants of sporty cars lending credibility to a line of successful low-end competition sports cars which used parts from the British automotive parts bin.

Photo courtesy TVRCCNA

TVR Jomar by Ray Saidel

29

The Griffith Years

As the 1954 calendars were being hung on the wall TVR changed their chassis design to a multi-tubular setup fitted with independent suspension and covered it with a custom designed fiberglass body. The TVR sports car was now being sold on a regular basis in England.

The predecessor to the Grantura model of the TVR had come into focus in 1956 and was powered with the very reliable and competitive Coventry Climax engine. This chassis design began to make its way across the pond after coupling with Ray Saidel, the USA distributor, who began mounting a body shell on the chassis giving birth to the Jomar model. This design was the one that mostly gave way to the Grantura model designation.

Since the Griffith is a direct descendant and outgrowth of the Grantura Mark III, the finer points of the history of TVR will be left to the historians of that marque.

After Jack bought out Lou Benny's half of the business partnership at White-Griffith Ford in the early sixties he combined the Ford dealership with a Jaguar franchise on the side. Within a short time, according to Jack, he got the notion to produce a dealer-prepared, high performance option which became the foundation for the Griffith Sprint idea.

Late in 1961 Ford dropped the idea of their "Y" block design V-8 powerplants, the 232, 272, 292 and 312 cid engines, and introduced their new small block, the 221 and 260-inch lightweights. This design, commonly known as the "Windsor" family of Ford engine blocks, was to eventually translate into the very successful 5.0 liter or 302 inch engine.

Editor's note: As of this printing that Windsor block still hasn't caved to the next generation of Dearborn iron and is still a sought-after favorite of the high performance crowd.

At first it was planted into the engine bay of the mid-sized Ford Fairlane but eventually was shoehorned into Ford's entry-level econo-car, the 1963 Falcon.

The Griffith Years

Nineteen sixty-one and sixty-two were busy years. Dick Monnich, a promoter and salesman from Levittown on Long Island who was involved in amateur SCCA club racing with a team that had been campaigning an AC Bristol, had been hanging around the Griffith Ford shop. He was interested in seeing what was going on and one project caught his eye. Jack Griffith was preparing to test the high performance waters with a variant of one of Henry Ford's cars, the Falcon Sprint with Roger Teck as the project mechanic/fabricator.

Those who were close to the center of the activity there said that Monnich saw the Griffith Sprint project as a possible contender for a Land Speed Record at Daytona Beach. He was said to have been shopping the idea of possibly making Jack Griffith into another Carroll Shelby.

Since Jack Griffith was a dealer whose facility had been utilized by Chrysler Corporation to set up the 1955 Plymouth for the assault on a class record on the Daytona Beach speed trials Monnich was possibly looking for his spot in the limelight.

Photo courtesy Jack Griffith collection

Jack Griffith's A-Production 289 Cobra

Griffith had signed on to become a Cobra dealer getting his cars from Ed Hugus, a car dealer from Pittsburgh who was the east coast distributor for the Shelby marque.

The Griffith Years

At about the same time, Bob Brown, Jr. was racing a Corvette out of his dad's dealership, Robert Chevrolet in Hicksville but as the Cobra's reputation grew as a 'Vette killer on the track, the younger Brown was now trying to get his dad to get a Cobra for him to drive in competition.

One of Bobby's high school chums, Roger Teck, had been racing his own Corvette on the local tracks for a couple of seasons along with Bobby and in '62 he was asked to tune and maintain Bobby's Corvette for some road racing competition.

Photo courtesy Jack Griffith collection
Jack Griffith driving his Cobra in the pits

When Jack offered Bobby a ride in a street version of the Cobra at Bridgehampton race circuit Jack said that he just couldn't get him out of the seat. The next step was a natural. Jack got Carroll Shelby on the phone and ordered the race-prepped Cobra.

"Carroll Shelby helped me as much as he could," Griffith said when he referred to the relationship that the two enjoyed. "We met once again in the late Eighties at one of the Daytona 500 races."

The Griffith Years

According to Griffith, Bobby was a good driver but he could tend to be a bit reckless and making the car last for an entire race was becoming more difficult all the time.

Bobby eventually lost his dream ride in the Cobra and Jack put Bob Johnson in his place for a short time. That was, until the day that Dick Monnich took Mark Donohue to meet Griffith.

Mark had gotten his start in automobile racing under the guidance of Walt Hansgen and an import car dealer from New Jersey named Lew Schulz.

According to Lew, Mark Donohue drove one of Lew's TVRs at Lime Rock Park in 1962 and 1963 and also co-drove with Gerry Sagerman in a works TVR at Sebring for Ken Richardson in 1962. On one trip there, Mark won five races in one day and each time he started from the scratch, or last, position.

As Mark continued his winning record Schulz offered Mark his first "sponsorship" for racing an Elva Courier which Mark had bought from Lew and history was about to be written. Mark would go on to break and set new records in whatever he drove and it didn't go unnoticed.

photo courtesy Virginia International Raceway
Walt Hansgen accepting President's Cup from Gen. Curtis LeMay, 1961

The Griffith Years

Mark, who had won thirteen of his first fifteen races under Lew Schulz's sponsorship, had been successfully driving Walt Hansgen's MGB in competition. He also co-drove with Walt finishing 12th in a Mecom-owned Ferrari at the 12 hours of Sebring.

Photo courtesy Jack Griffith collection

1964 Griffith Sprint prototype under construction

The Griffith Sprint project was getting done in between races and Roger Teck had his hands full. The engine chosen for the car was one of the new 289 high performance engines being offered as an option in the 1964 Ford Fairlanes, not unlike the power plant of the Shelby AC Cobra.

Photo courtesy Jack Griffith collection

1964 Griffith Sprint Prototype

The Griffith Sprint would have special wheels, a 9-inch Ford rear end along with some custom gauges and gee-gaws separating it from its weaker-kneed brethren.

Rumor has it that on one particular day late in 1963 when Monnich drove the Grantura into the Griffith shop it was like any other morning. Jack and Dick sat down over a cup of coffee to chat about cars among other things and the conversation was said to have swung over to the little TVR and the lightweight Ford family of engines; the 221, 260 and 289 so they decided to look over the prospect of making them work as a team.

Roger Teck had been already working on the Griffith Sprint and it was decided at that time to go ahead with the prototype "TVR-Griffith" project.

George Clark, a young and aggressive mechanic who had been working at Frank Dominiani's hot rod shop on Merrick Road in Valley Stream on the south shore of Long Island, was introduced into the Griffith shop by his friend, Roger Teck.

Both of these talented mechanics were working together on the two cars but fate would take a twist in the story. As George became more involved with the prototype, Roger reportedly fell out of favor with Monnich and Clark was given the nod to build the prototype Griffith. Roger was history.

The time for growth for the Griffith was at hand and the direction of that growth was something that one member of the organization was having a difficult time with.

The ball game had started and Dick Monnich owned the baseball.

The Griffith Years

three

the Prototype

"..There were lots of people, maybe more than twenty, who said that they helped to build the car but they sure never brought me any coffeee."
George Clark

When George Clark got the go-ahead to start the production of the Griffith prototype he was in the midst of taking over the Griffith Sprint project from Roger Teck.

Roger had been working with Jack Griffith to get Jack's new project off the drawing board and inserted into the high performance market, a muscular '64 Falcon Sprint.

There was a spot behind Dave Schineller's service manager's position in the Ford service shop that became the hallowed ground where the Griffith was born. With a gestation period of about six weeks George Clark had two cars to bring into this world for Jack.

The Griffith Sprint was a concept car. In the early and mid Sixties, a few car dealers of mixed persuasion would put together a concept car, one that would be an outgrowth of a production vehicle, dress it up, hang a few catalog speed options from the body and give it a nickname or product name and go racing.

These projects would engender such dramatic cars as the Tasca 427 Mustang, the Motion 427 Camaro and Chicago's own and very successful Nickey (replete the backwards "k" in the trademark) Chevrolet Camaros and Chevelles. These were specialty cars that would be built and prepped by individual dealerships in a seemingly unending assault on the quarter-mile drag strips and Saturday night cruises around the country.

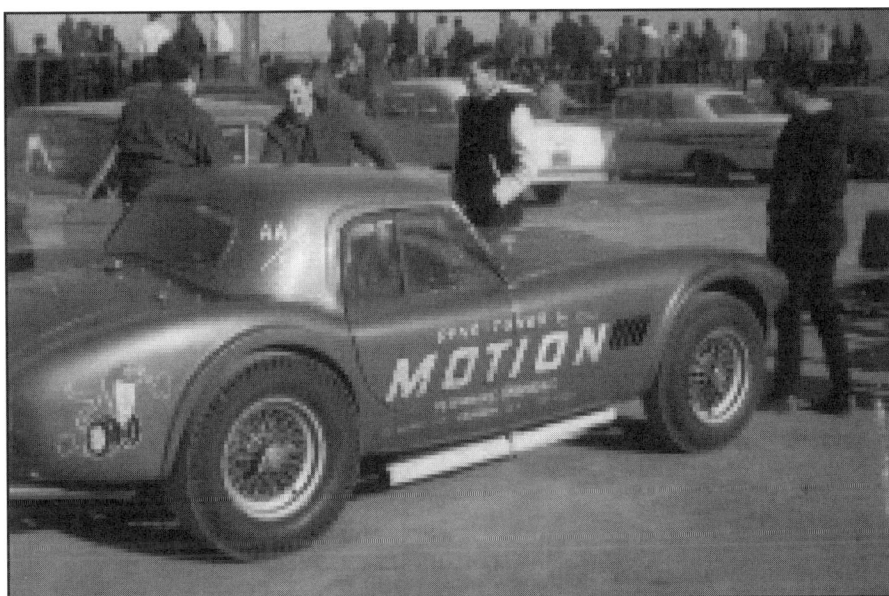

Photo by Mike Mooney

Motion Cobra at New York National Speedway

At one time a very successful Shelby 289 AC Cobra brutalized the class records in the NHRA AA/Sports category and was tuned by Motion Performance on Sunrise Highway in Baldwin, Long Island, New York. The driver was noted for pulling the front wheels off the ground out of the chute and holding them airborne through a power-shift into second gear while blowing the doors off anything that dared to compete.

Well, Jack wanted to put his imprint on the industry with the Griffith Sprint.

He foresaw the marketing viability of high performance and the plan was to take an early-production '64 Ford Falcon Sprint, two-door hardtop with the factory 260-inch small block. He would then massage it with a 289 high performance engine, put some shiny wire wheels on each corner and add a dash of performance dashboard instrumentation.

Choosing an engine was relatively easy. Ford had just introduced the 271 horsepower version of the 289 cubic inch engine that was touted as being the same one that was powering the Cobra.

Willie Seitz, a machinist and metal fabricator who was known for producing some fine cylinder head work, was called on to work his magic on blueprinting the engine. The heads were made to flow-match the cam, an Engle #324 grind, and the necessary machining was completed to make the engine to lean more towards the wild side of civilized.

The car was planned to be sporting four-wheel disk brakes, well ahead of its time, that were fitted to the Ford suspension by Willie. The front brakes were taken from the Jaguar parts bin (remember that Jack also hung the Jag sign out front), the rear brakes were of some racing variety and Willie made them work.

Before either of the cars could be marketed there had to be a blessing come down the pipe from Dearborn. Jack Griffith was making sure that he could get his painting on the canvas and George was his artist.

Being the ever ready agent-in-waiting, Jack Griffith scored a double-header. He would become a Ford performance dealer and also market the new Shelby AC Cobra.

As the four-cylinder engine was removed from the bay of the TVR Grantura Mk. III for fitting the Ford small block into the engine compartment of this little British immigrant Jack was acting as a holdover agent for Carroll Shelby.

The Griffith Years

He was responsible for making the contact at the piers in New York, transporting them to Hicksville and storing them as they awaited the over-the-road trailers from California for their trip to Los Angeles, California.

While he was building the prototype in the back room at Griffith Ford Jack had Cobras in his showroom, a "Griffith Sprint" being constructed in the shop and a pile of Cobra bodies taking up valuable work space. Roger Teck had indicated that at one time there were as many as nine AC bodies waiting inside one of the Griffith dealership buildings for their three-thousand mile trek west.

Photo by Mike Mooney

289 AC Cobra in Griffith showroom in May, 1964
Note: This Cobra would eventually be sold to Darryl Green, an illustrator for Bantam Books.
Griffith Ford Sales Mgr. Joe Quinn sitting on desk behind Cobra and Pete Elardo behind Fairlane

Both cars were completed in November of 1963 and now they were on their way to Dearborn, Michigan for inspection. George Clark, Jack Griffith and Dick Monnich towed the cars north for an audience with the Ford brass.

Time was wasting and in order to firm up the whole package he needed to "kiss the ring" in Dearborn. Jack had these two cars on the front burner and George Clark had his hands busy working towards a deadline.

The Griffith Years

Lee Iacocca was in on the meeting as Ford executives went over both of the cars with a magnifying glass to see if it would fit into the corporate portfolio.

Ford eventually would be happy to give Jack the corporate "thumbs up" for the little shave-tail with the big Ford powerplant but when Mr. Iacocca took the New York threesome into the dark chambers three levels beneath the street and flooded the room with lights, the success car of the "Sixties" was shown center stage... the Mustang. It turns out that Jack's "Griffith Sprint" would be in direct competition with the soon-to-be-introduced pony car and the approval for the project was denied by Ford.

Jack and his entourage were batting .500 and that ain't bad. After a few days in Dearborn they headed back to Long Island with a plan. The Griffith Motorcar Corporation was now more than a dream. All that had to be done was to get the approval in writing from Ford.

Now Jack had to make the big decision. It was either sell Fords or build Griffiths and it was time to sell the Griffith Ford dealership and concentrate on the new car. Over the winter of '63-'64 all the pieces were being put into place for the production and make the move from car dealer to car manufacturer.

TVR was put on notice. Jack Griffith, through Dick Monnich, told TVR in Britain that they had to supply their entire production of bodies and chassis for the Griffith project. TVR was a company that was at one time producing five bodies a month. They tried to increase that figure to six a week but the figure of fifteen or more bodies a week was a staggering logistical obstacle that had to be overcome.

There was also the contract to be signed with Ford to become the supplier of "industrial" engines and transmissions for the Griffith. All of the pieces were coming together. Jack made the commitment and leased a commercial building on Eileen Way just off Jericho Turnpike in the bustling New York City bedroom community of Syosset in Nassau County on Long Island. The Griffith was about to become a part of the American high-performance automotive scene.

The Griffith Years

What Jack wanted built was an entry level cruiser for the masses who could dust off a fair part of the street competition without breaking the bank. Lightweight, potent and affordable; a great combination when the average annual salary was in the vicinity of high fours to the mid-eights.

Now he had a chance to do the deed and in the shadow of Carroll Shelby's Cobra project. Since Griffith Ford had already signed on to becoming the first Cobra distributor/dealer on the east coast it was a natural for him to test the waters.

Dick Monnich was busy making sure that Griffith would have his TVR bodies to make the transition from a mild-mannered little British sporty car into a fire-breathing, manic-depressive, psychotic and macadam-destroying slingshot but some changes were soon to be made.

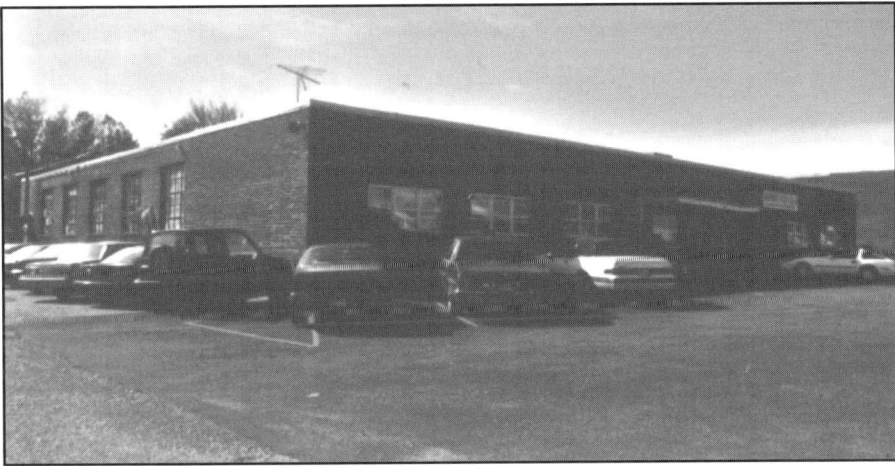

photo by Mike Mooney

141 Eileen Way, Syosset, N.Y.

Prior to the first body being delivered to the Griffith Ford shop, Roger was "out" and George was "in" for the project. Just behind the service manager's position Jack had designated an area that would be not only the location for assembling the unfinished Sprint but also where the prototype would get to wear its new suit.

41

The Griffith Years

Initial measurements were made when the TVR arrived and George was trying to put all of the basic race engineering practices into making it all work. Engine location, front and rear mount heights, cooling, electrics and general all-around fit was being checked.

In the meantime, Griffith line mechanic, John Fisher would keep watch on what was going on across the repair bay in the shop. He and his brother-in-law, service manager Dave Schineller, would take a moment or two to talk with George as he tried to make it all fit together.

"They never evaluated the car," said John. "The one problem with the whole assembly was that they never evaluated what would work with everything else in the car."

"Out in California, Carroll Shelby had an entire engineering team to test and try out every change in the development of the Cobra," according to Roger Teck. "They had Bill Stroppe on the west coast and Holman-Moody on the east coast to shake everything out in their racing programs. Griffith didn't do any of that."

As George and his wife, Karen, worked on putting the car together, Karen would learn to weld. She was taught to "tack weld" the header pipes in position for installation and George would do the finishing touches. It was at this time that the weird front-exiting exhaust manifolds were developed so as to clear the engine, chassis and body work.

In later years as more and more facts came to the surface the hunt for the original prototype was on and it all came to bear by accident.

Each year for several years running, the TVR Car Club of North America (TVRCCNA) has sponsored an annual gathering of the beasts of Hoo Hill and beyond. At one of the more recent outings we had been listening to stories related us by a Griffith, or so thought, owner who had a weird type of car. It was not as pretty as many of the cars that were assembled on the parking lot in New Jersey in fact, it wasn't even there.

The Griffith Years

Joe Gerardi, the man who had owned this "ugly duckling" had not done too much to it in the twenty or so years that he had treasured the car since it appeared to be in limbo. The Griffith Club trackers agreed that it was some sort of Griffith. The TVR Club allowed it to be part of the rota since it was, undoubtedly, a TVR but that's where it all seemed to end.

Since the car had been treated to some unweildly body parts, bumps and additions, it really didn't resemble a "stock" Griffith. It was also in need of some serious restoration but Gerardi was not sure which way to go. Was it a "wannabe" Griffith or a surreal TVR?

photo by Ryan Brophy

The Saratoga Gathering, August, 2002
L to R: Front row- Dave Schineller, Karen Bocsusis, Len Bailey, Russ Rogers
Back row: Mike Mooney, Roger Teck, George Clark, John Fisher, Willie Seitz

In August of 2002, a meeting was arranged for several members of the Griffith crew and brought together at the Saratoga (New York) Automobile Museum. Most of them had not seen each other since the company went to motor heaven.

The Griffith Years

There was George Clark, Willie Seitz, Len Bailey, Dave Schineller, John Fisher, Karen (Clark) Bocsusis, Roger Teck and Mike Mooney. Russ Rogers brought his beautiful Series 200 #153 Griffith along for "eyewash" at the meeting.

During the five days that we had to spend with George Clark, who had built the prototype, the information was forged on paper and on tape as to what really went into building the car.

Now we fast-forward two months later and we are listening to Joe Gerardi explaining all of the symetrics and asymetrics of his car, VIN (Vehicle Identification Number) 200-5-000. Three Zeroes! No wonder the Griffith Club had put a large question mark in front of this entry but that was soon to be laid to rest.

As Joe tried to describe the various abnormalities of his "000" car, we started to hear a lot of the same things that we had listened to in detail only a couple of months earlier.

photos by Joe Gerardi

Joe Gerardi's unusual and customized Series 200-4-000

When Joe was asked if he had spoken to George Clark he told us that he was still waiting for a response back but had had no personal contact. With that information in hand and with the help of modern technology the two were finally united via a wireless phone call.

The two chatted on for about ten minutes, George asking the questions and Joe filling in the blanks. When the call was over, Joe handed us the phone, his eyes glazed over and his hand shaking.

The Griffith Years

After the dust had settled, George had only one statement. "We found it!" With all assurances that George had taken the time to recall for the club to verify, Joe Gerardi learned that this poor misshapen lump of fiberglass, aluminum and steel was actually the first Griffith made. According to George Clark, we had finally located the prototype.

Of note was that the prototype car, a maroon car and the first-ever Griffith, sporting a VIN of 200-4-000, was said to have been originally sold to Markland Gates of Sunnyvale, California by Charles Stuart Motors, 2757 NW 36 Street, in Miami, Florida.

During this period Jack Griffith was planning for the future and seeking out a buyer for the dealership. He had to make the decision to either build Griffiths or to sell Fords. He chose the former.

The Griffith Years

four

Eileen Way

**"..If a man look sharply and attentively, he shall see fortune;
for though she be blind, yet she is not invisible."**
Sir Francis Bacon

Not too far from the Griffith Ford workshop on Routes 106/107 in Hicksville stirred the bustling little town of Syosset, an upscale community that bordered the "Gold Coast" luxury of the North Shore of this toney section of Long Island.

Jack found a site with a 10,000 square foot building that was just right to get the project on track. 141 Eileen Way, just south of Jericho Turnpike, the address that would now be fixed to the letterheads of the Griffith Car Corporation, became home. Spring of '64 was just around the corner and so was the new Series 200 Griffith.

The anxiety factor was at a high pitch as the plans started to materialize for the first Griffith motorcar factory. Workers were busy moving in their tools, carpenters were readying the racks, welders and fabricators were scurrying back and forth making sure that the assembly line would be ready for the first draft of TVR bodies that came in from the United Kingdom.

Contrary to many of the movies filmed about the glamorous suburban denizens who used their Long Island addresses for their unprinted social calling cards, there were normal communities that many of the middle class families called home and Syosset was one of these.

photo by Mike Mooney

Rear of 141 Eileen Way, Syosset, N.Y.

Located just west of the bustling town of Huntington and not too far from Hicksville, Syosset offered a location that would not only provide an excellent location in one of the newly-built industrial parks but it would also be accessible to the many new post-Korean war veterans who would be making Long Island their home and workplace.

George Clark had to move his growing tool collection and materials to the shop, the front office had to be set up to accommodate the ever-growing list of requirements of the fledgling factory and plans for the brochures and publicity for the new car would have to be readied.

Number 141 Eileen Way was now a bee hive of activity. Dealers would have to be signed on for the sales program and a sales manager would have to be put in place to make sure that orders could be filled. Early company records are just about impossible to find but some of the letters from those early days, Donald F. Millager, who sold Jack his first sports car back in 1948, was named Griffith sales manager in March of 1964.

With an introduction date of March 29, 1964, the press release written by Paul Elisha noted, **"The Griffith, America's Newest Sports Car Is Introduced At The Internat'l Auto Show"** and the race was on.

With an expected retail price of $3,995.00, the Griffith was touted as one of the fastest and least expensive sports cars on the market. The press release illustrated that **"…based upon his evaluation of the initial response, (Jack) Griffith said he expected the company's first year's production of 750 cars to be sold out by summer."**

In the company-produced suggested price list showed the standard production car would include a "…195 HP Ford-Cobra, 289 cu. in. engine; fully Synchromized (sic) Ford four speed manual transmission; Full (sic) instrumentation;" etc. and at the sale price of $3995.00, a dealer would stand to make $600.00.

If a buyer wanted to have a 289 cid 271 bhp (HiPo) engine, that would add $495.00, a veritable bargain in the days of the traffic-light Grand Prix. On any given Saturday night, for about a total of a little over $4,400, you could blow the doors off anything that was available on the road in '64 and then drive it to work on Monday! Given the right massaging, the car could out-Cobra Carroll Shelby.

As mentioned, Dick Monnich held the import rights to the TVR car and he had ideas of his own as to which direction he would most likely imagine that this new car company should travel. With his limited experience in SCCA-type club racing, Monnich immediately saw the Griffith as a potential record-breaker, a headliner, a winner and a great springboard onto the international car racing scene.

The Griffith Years

Editor's note: Given the fact that Jack Griffith's Plymouth-DeSoto dealership was blessed with tuning and preparing the '56 Plymouth for a land speed record. Monnich reportedly imagined that, with the help of Jack Griffith and his high performance ideas, he could eventually not only be a star on the sports car tracks of the country and, perhaps, the world, but could also launch an attempt at shattering some of the world speed records.

An idea was hatched that with Mark Donohue winning in Jack's Cobra, that an attempt to build a "prototype" car with Mark at the helm would be put on the table.

A "topless" version of the Grantura/200 body series was being designed. It would sport an ultra-light body, a special chassis and along with several engineering ideas that would probably sift down into production. More information on this car will be covered later in the book.

The Research & Development (R&D) effort was ramping up for eventual production changes for the upcoming Series 400 and 600.

It was in mid-March that Jack Griffith got the word from Ford giving the final approval for Jack's request for engines and transmissions for the new car and a month later with everyone at the ready, the production line started to move.

Oddly enough, in mid-April the first car off the production line would probably be one of the last ones sold. The story of chassis number 001E, which will be covered in a later chapter, was to become the center of controversy when the list of chassis was compiled years later.

photo courtesy Jack Griffith collection

Griffith Sprint surrounded by a gaggle of Series 200s

With TVR shuffling to get the maximum number of cars on the boat for the trip across the pond, another wrinkle in the production line showed up. Even though the basic Griffith body design was based on the TVR Grantura Mk. III, a few minor design changes were made to differentiate the two.

First was the large bulge in the hood and another was the mounting location for the license plate. In England, license plates were of different dimensions, wider and less stout in height compared to the narrower and taller U.S. plates, so the Griffith had an indentation with a faired lower section so as to accommodate the different plates.

It can be noted that some of the early Griffith Series 200 bodies did have an amalgamation of different design affixations as the TVR Grantura fiberglass body production shop formed up for the transition. The air vent holes on the side of the tilt-nose bonnet in the early body molds were said to have been quite different from body to body that even the Griffith line had to improvise with the insert trim.

photo courtesy Motor Cars Illustrated

George Clark, center, working on Griffith engine installation

As production continued and a standardized body with its specific identification designs, the side trim, engine-compartment vent, foot box fresh air vents, fender trim and license plate mounting, the cars became more uniform in appearance.

In production form, the excessive heat that was being generated by the Ford engine actually forced the change in the design of this air exit hole at the side of the hinged bonnet. According to George Clark, this design did little to repair the inherent overheating difficulty.

Just above the rear wheels at the top of the fender well opening a small flare on the Mk. III was also changed. Rather than make it the straight double-ended upper accent line, the flare was altered to continue to follow the fender flare line and continue down to the bottom of the fender well opening. This change, though consistent on the later Series 200s, some of the early bodies still bore the Grantura double-ended "bullet" design.

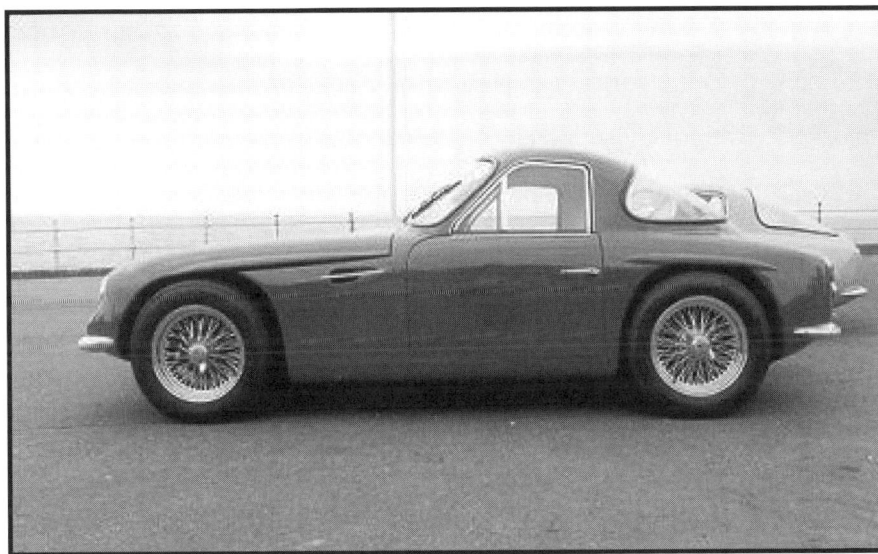

photo courtesy TVRCCNA

TVR Grantura Mk. III

Oddly, with the exception of the original prototype, s/n 200-4-000, Griffith that George Clark built in the shop area of Griffith's Hicksville auto dealership, the first three TVR bodies that Monnich delivered were Grantura Mk III units.

These three Grantura-bodied cars were given the chassis numbers of 015, 016 and 017 in the normal production sequence with Griffith Vehicle

Identification Number (VIN) plates and were possibly the only three non-Griffith bodied cars and were probably a tad lighter than the rest.

These three cars are often referred to as the "lightweights" since the production Griffith bodies were given just a little more fiberglass than their predecessors. They were also fitted with a lower chassis position engines mounts, as in the prototype, and had the "British-style" license plate frames and the rear fender treatment though other older designs could be found on some of the early Series 200s.

As production continued the engineering glitches began to work their way out of the system. Willie Seitz would be given the chore of exorcising the resident evils out of the cars and he usually did the trick.

When production started, Peter Dodge and Joe DeTore were two of the first factory workers to be hired. Peter was assigned to be the car transporter driver who picked up the cars at the New York docks and doubled as one of the factory workers. Both of these lads had gone to school together in Levittown and DeTore was already earning his reputation as a hot shot mechanic.

A young intern, Jim Ketcher, who joined the team three months into production, took over Peter's job of picking up the cars at the docks with the company truck, a rickety old '62 or '63 Ford cab-over, probably an F-600, which was designed to take no more than four bodies at a time and had one of those hand-cranked winches.

"To start off with," Ketcher said, "without the engine in place the front ends would come off the boat with both front tires looking at each other. We couldn't pull them by hand so we had to bring a pair of vise grips with us to un-adjust the tie rods so that we could just get them to the car carrier."

Jim said that on one trip, a short-lived and unnamed employee of Griffith had done something to anger the dock workers prior to Jim's employment. When Jim came aboard about three months into the Griffith production period his initial trip was met with a lock-out at the dock. The stevedores would have to push each rolling body to the gate and Jim and his helper would then have to push it to the car carrier after they made the steering adjustment.

According to Jim, as a note of interest, he said that many current Griffith owners could probably look for vise-grip teeth marks on the tie rod and know how they got there. This was just one of the "beauty marks" to show up on the Griffith.

Once back at the factory the bodies were rolled up on to the assembly ramps and readied for the powertrain installation. Crated Ford engine and transmission assemblies were rolled over to the line and hoisted above the engine bay. But not before one very important adjustment.

When George Clark installed the first 289 into the prototype at Griffith Ford the engine mounting location was about three inches lower in the chassis than it would be in the production car. When the final engine placement was selected, the starter motor was found to be blocked by a chassis member.

Sitting atop one of the tool boxes in the shop was a sixteen-pound sledge hammer that was engaged in a chassis-slamming ceremony. Now the engine and the chassis could coexist after the use of this "duty sledgehammer." Most every chassis in the early production was blessed with a "hand-smash fit" at the factory.

More production problems started to multiply. The first few Griffiths were fitted with the "Red Engines," a group of six engines that were probably pulled from the pile of industrial "spec" engines and, when installed in the Griffiths, proved themselves to be powerless beyond a 4,000 RPM rev range. "They just laid down and died, when we put the coals to them," according to Jim Ketcher.

George Clark and Roger Teck concurred. According to some of the factory workers the problem was traced back to the Ford shop. The powertrains were ordered as "industrial engines" as they should have been, but what was delivered was a gaggle of underpowered, possibly marine units, that were totally unusable as street fighters.

The Griffith Years

Clark then hit another brick wall in July of '64. In the hot and humid Long Island summer, George had been trying to get a better radiator fitted for the car. As designed for a four-cylinder car rolling over the roads of the cooler U.K, the factory radiator was overwhelmed by the larger, higher-heat producing Ford 289 and it proved to be totally inadequate.

The prototype had been fitted with an efficient Harrison aluminum radiator that worked well but Dick Monnich would not pass the problem nor the fix onto the factory in England. According to Clark, Dick did not think that the refit was necessary. This was just one more in the several clashes that Clark had with Monnich and would definitely not be the last.

That same month the Griffiths were coming back with electrical problems. Ford had originally fitted the 289s with a 55 amp/hr. alternator but since it clashed with a part of the chassis the alternator was ditched and replaced with a very minimal 30 amp./hr. generator. As an industrial engine is ordered the customer usually specifies the required components. The electrical power requirements were bypassed and the Griffith was sufferring.

photo courtesy Jack Griffith collection

Rolling chassis and optional equipment in Griffith showroom

As it was designed, most Griffiths came off the assembly line with an optional (yes, optional!) heater, an AM-band radio, coil/spark ignition, electric windshield wipers, radiator fan, road lights, an electric fan and an electric fuel pump all drawing current from the battery. It had to be replenished or the car would stop running.

Again, Clark would beg to have the necessary changes but this, too, fell on deaf ears. One story that George would recall was of a customer who opted to pick up his new Griffith at the factory late in the afternoon on a hot, sweltering, rainy day in the summer of 1964.

As he left the overhead door at the rear of 141 Eileen Way, the new owner flicked on the headlights, the windshield wipers, the defroster fan and drove off into the evening muck.

Within an hour, this now-drenched and enraged driver was back. Pounding on the door, he was screaming that he wanted his money back. The car stopped running down the road and couldn't start! It was then that he had to confront a glaring situation of the necessity of budgeting his electrical appliances or adding a more powerful generator or the new alternator.

From their arrival on the docks, the rolling bodies came into the factory, the fuel tanks were removed and repaired, the half-shaft bolts were removed and replaced with case-hardened items and now cars were finally being built.

Tensions were rising as fast as the orders were coming in. The production line quickly turned from being just for assembly to one that more resembled an after-market repair shop.

Expansion was peeking around the corner and it would be a mighty sharp curve for Griffith to maneuver through.

The Griffith Years

five

Old Country Road

"Nothing great was ever achieved without enthusiasm."
Ralph Waldo Emerson

Following its debut at the 1964 New York Auto Show, the publicity stirring about the new Griffith brought inquiries about this underweight and anorexic sports car. Figures were showing that the Cobra could be unseated from its position atop the "quick" ladder.

It was only coincidental that the new Sunbeam Tiger, the Rootes Group's handy little all-steel bodied, Ford-powered version of the Alpine, would be introduced but it was only equipped with the 164 bhp 260 cubic inch small block and it weighed nearly a half-ton greater than the Griffith. I guess that Ford had to find someplace to get rid of the left-over and outdated 260s.

Dick Monnich was reported to have spouted to "Ol' Shel", Carroll Shelby, at one meeting within the Ford corporate walls that the Griffith would "bury" the Cobra at Sebring. Not nice!

Griffith Roadster rear spoiler and special body treatment

Monnich knew well that he had a potential secret weapon being readied within the walls of the Griffith factory, Mark Donohue's topless, lightweight racer. He was waiting for the special body to be delivered from England, a Cobra killer, which was planned to not only bring international notice to the car but also boost the potential sales of a TVR-based car. Monnich was looking for the pot of gold and Jack Griffith was building the rainbow.

Gene Balmes racing in the Griffith Roadster

The Roadster and the plaid car would reportedly be sold along with the repainted "plaid" car to a Ford dealer in Michigan where they were both strengthened and modified. They were then raced successfully for several years in the midwest in regional sports car competition

This was not the only news that would come from the Griffith organization. Mark Donohue had been winning on the track with Jack Griffith's Cobra and earned his first national victory at Virginia International Raceway in early '64. Then after making some neat adjustments to Walt Hansgen's MGB, won the 500-miler at Bridgehampton on the east end of Long Island.

photo from Internet

Gene Balmes driving the repainted "plaid" car

The winning streak that Mark was enjoying while he was driving for Jack brought him into the national limelight earning him a seat for the 12 Hours of Sebring. Not in a Griffith but in a John Mecom-owned Ferrari 275 LM. Monnich must have been devastated! He was never going to be able to carry out the challenge that he offered to Carroll Shelby.

George Clark, who had been "wrenching" Mark's Cobra while he was racing for Griffith, was not in on the Hansgen deal but he would retain the friendship. George had his hands full trying to exorcise the demons out of the Griffith.

Clark had been bucking heads with Dick Monnich more often now and Jack had to smooth away some of the friction. With his experience working on serious racing cars George knew what was needed to make the car work but was getting no help from the factory connection.

Patience was growing thin and in November of 1964, George packed up his tools and left the organization letting Jack know that as long as Dick was still on board, he would no longer work on the Griffith.

Jack was in a quandary knowing that Monnich was his pipeline to the TVR body availability; the definitive "Catch 22." Owing to the fact that Jack very rarely went behind the front office doors, Monnich often was seen by those around him as the "boss" at the factory. In fact, Dick Triano was production manager and Jack brought his brother-in-law, Don Johnson, in from the west coast to keep the books straight.

George went back to work at the Ford dealership, out of the way of his problems on the production line at Eileen Way. Occasionally, Jack would often call on John Fisher, a savvy line mechanic at the former Griffith Ford dealership, in a way to get some additional help. John would lend his experience and help but told Jack on many occasions that he would not leave his position at Ford.

Now that Mark had been offered a nicer ride than what Monnich could offer, tempers were on edge but a new Series model of Griffith was being readied. In England TVR was working with an improved body style which would become the base design for the Griffith Series 400.

The building at Eileen Way was already showing signs of too much growth and Jack had to seek out newer quarters. Not wanting to move too far away since many of the work force were locals, he found a newer factory location and in a more visible neighborhood.

Summer had passed, sales numbers were growing and there seemed to be as many directions to go as there were members of the organization. Lew Schulz had sold his dealership in New Jersey, relaxed for a few months and then signed on as sales manager for Griffith.

The Griffith Years

Just south of the newly-finished Long Island Expressway at Exit 49 in Plainview, 1478 Old Country Road would become the new home of the Griffith Motorcar Corporation. Workers feverishly worked on the move from Eileen Way to set up the new production facilities.

Lew Schulz had the feel for salesmanship as Mark had the feel for the road. The motoring press scribes were quick to give their driving impressions of the little car and each story was as different as there were colors in the kaleidoscope. Some reported that the car was managable and roadworthy yet there were those who proclaimed that a Griffith parked in a garage was more dangerous than a motorcycle at full chat at Daytona Motor Speedway.

No matter, the 200-Series cars were selling like hotcakes and leaving the factory doors in numbers nearing 20 per month. Not only was Jack elated with the sales figures but he also had a new model to introduce. The Series 400 was ready to take on what the 200 couldn't handle, or was it?

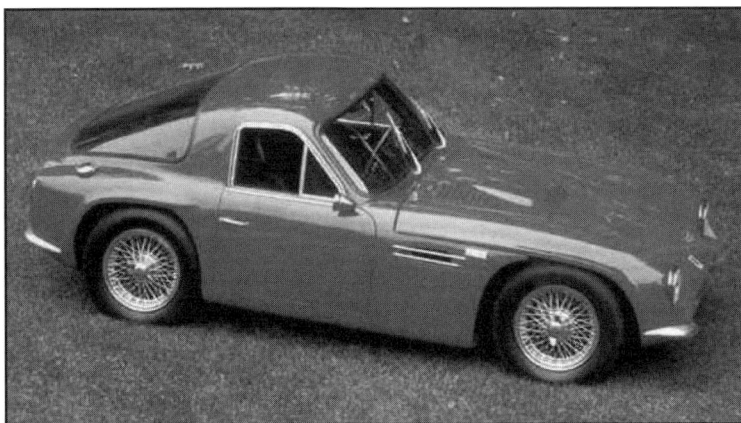

photo courtesy Griffith Car Club

Griffith series 400-5-003

Late in 1964 the news media announced the new Series 400. This model would be equipped with a standard 289 Ford High Performance engine, the engine that enjoyed the lineage of the powerplant that occupied the engine bay of the Cobra. The Griffith was reported to weigh in at a tick over 1700 lbs. and could take on the best that anyone could offer. But it was up to the factory to convince the masses.

The Griffith Years

The move to Old Country Road was timed perfectly for the introduction of the Series 400. The media were already reporting on the varying merits or curses of the Series 200 but no matter, the production fervor was set at a high pitch, but a few problems were lurking.

With a visible presence in the national and international magazines and print outlets note was taken by the United Auto Workers (UAW) that Griffith was not a union shop. This would be "new meat" for the union players. Plans were afoot to bring the employees at Griffith into the union fold.

At least one employee within the shop was reportedly handing out leaflets that were proclaiming the benefits of joining the UAW and it was more than a small concern for management.

Should a vote be forced by the factory workers and the shop become unionized, it would most likely create a slowing of the momentum that the introduction of this new car was enjoying and would also affect to the final cost of selling the car.

Jack Griffith did his best to keep in close touch with Dick Triano, the plant manager, for any information concerning the growth of the union intrusion although some of the former factory workers later said that Jack was unaware of the union intrusions.

According to some there, the union threat occupied no more than a temporary moment and that the employee who was responsible for distributing the leaflets was just about ignored or not well-liked by the rest of the workers.

Union threat or not, Griffith had to build and sell cars. Looking back a few years, in April of 1962 TVR founder, Trevor Wilkinson, left the company just prior to declaring bankruptcy. Its main supplier, Grantura Engineering Ltd., took over the facilities. The company was not on the best of financial footing and the contract with Jack Griffith was its major crutch. Without Griffith, TVR/Grantura would most likely not have survived that period in its history.

The Griffith Years

Just following Griffith's move into their new quarters a death knell was about to strike. Not the union nor the engineering or sales. It was a dock strike. The dockworkers union struck the entire east coast late in from December of 1964 and ran through April of '65, from Maine to the Gulf coast, the walkout bringing the import community to a halt.

Grantura Engineering was doing its best to supply the bodies but they could not be shipped to the US. A few more than fifty Series 400 bodies were barely out the door and the supply spigot was shut. Nothing was moving across the pond and any organization that relied on a "Just In Time" (JIT) delivery for production or sales would suffer and Griffith fit the form.

At one point Griffith attempted the expensive route of air transporting bodies but at that point it was just economically unfeasable and the idea was short-lived.

Cash flow at Griffith was just like any new business. If the sales are suddenly cut off the ready cash is needed for fixed costs and if there is nothing to replenish the coffers the well goes dry. This was a shallow well and there was no end in sight to the dock strike.

Creditors had to be satisfied, salaries had to be paid and cars had to be built but the cash flow wasn't there. Jack had to make some difficult decisions about the future of his dream. Sales manager, Lew Schulz related that shop manager Dick Triano had been instructed to release half of the factory workers and he had no idea how to make the cut.

As he contemplated several methods of drawing the line as to who stayed and who went he worried about the hardships that this decision would visit on the workers who had put their hearts into making the car succeed.

He finally relied on the clock to make the decision. Dick picked an arbritary time of the morning at which half of the work force arrived, used that moment as the cutting line and released those who came in the door after that ill-fated moment.

The Griffith Years

Editor's Note: When one former factory worker was interviewed for this book and told of that day's occurrence, he took a deep breath, slumped his head to his chest and expressed thanks for the information. Over the years he had thought that the cause of his being fired was due to something that he had done and held a deep resentment over the years about the incident. He was finally at peace with his former bosses.

Not only had the 400 been cut off at the knees with news of an impending TVR Grantura collapse, the soon-to-be Series 600 was affected. Since the outset of the Griffith idea, Jack had been planning future models to be introduced in rapid succession. In 1964, a series of new designs were introduced to the press as representations of future models. The drawing board yielded a couple of futuristic designs with sharp leading edges and gobs of slanted glass to whet the appetite of the sports-motoring public.

Though the final model of the Series 600 was a spectacular cross between a Ferrari and a Vignale, it didn't come even close to resembling the planned designs that were shown in early 1964. Jack Griffith wanted to proliferate the idea as the company would grow but the production line was screeching to a halt.

When news of the TVR collapse reached the States in the midst of the dock strike it was devastating and would put an end to all of Jack's plans. The Griffith Motorcar Corporation would suffer a mortal blow.

The Griffith Years

The Griffith Years

Griffith 200-5-123

Jack Griffith and Walt Hotchkiss with 200-6-001E

photo via Internet

Griffith Series 600

photo courtesy of Graham Povey

British Griffith on the track

photo courtesy Intermeccanica/Reisner

Intermeccanica Torino

photo courtesy of John & Chip Young

Series 200-5-181 under restoration

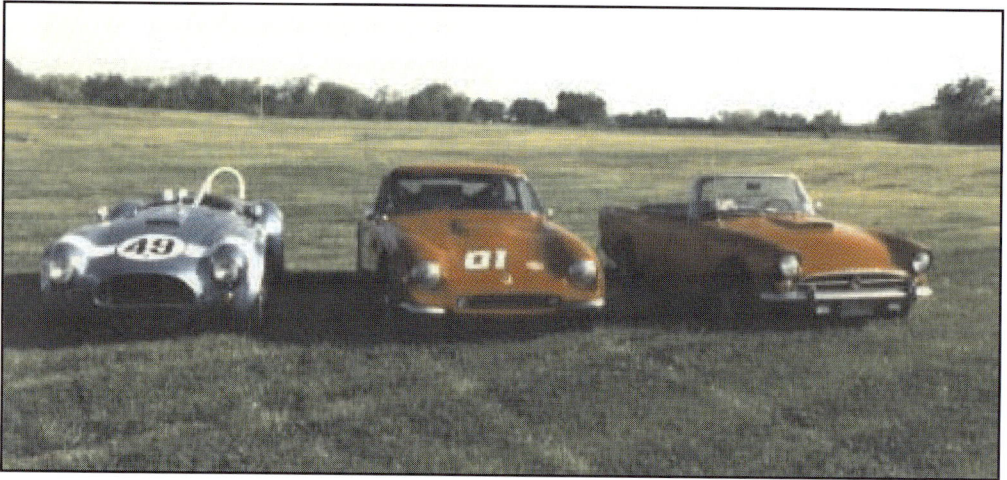

photo by Mike Mooney

**The Three Amigos at Summit Point - Fran Kress' Competition AC Cobra,
Walt Hotchkiss' 200-6-001E Griffith and Mike Mooney's Mk I Sunbeam Tiger**

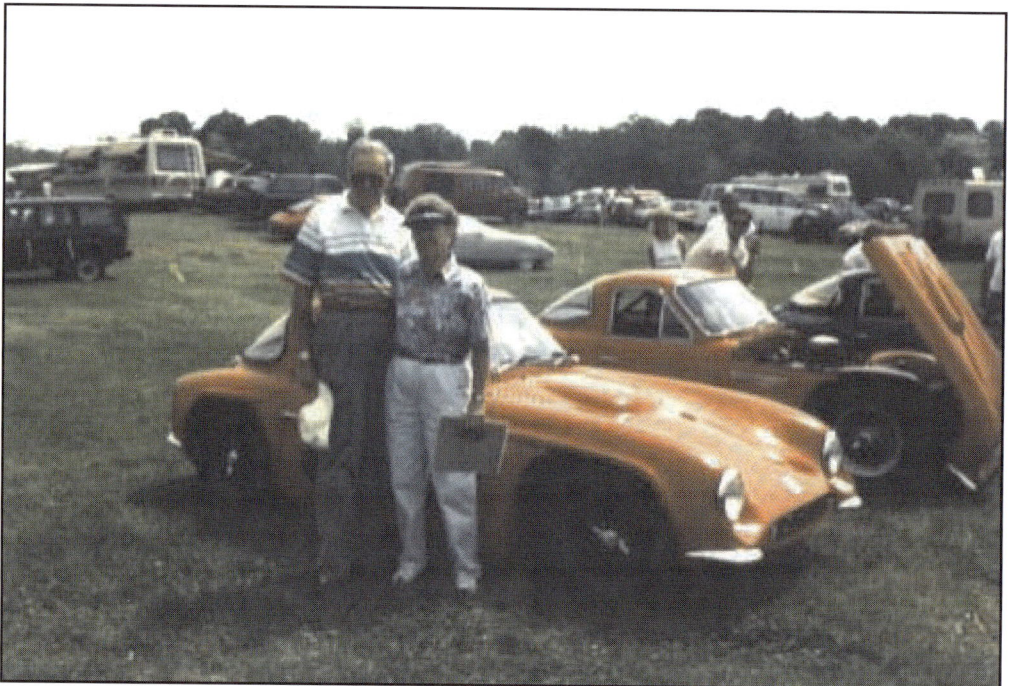

photo by Mike Mooney

Marge & Jack Griffith with one of their "children"

photo courtesy Jack Griffith collection

The Plaid car at the '65 New York Auto Show

photo courtesy Jack Griffith collection

The Griffith 600 at the '65 New York Auto Show

photo courtesy of Griffith Car Club

Series 200-5-058

photo courtesy of Hayes Harris

Griffith 200-5-011

photo courtesy of Griffith Car Club

Griffith 200-5-063

photo courtesy of Griffith Car Club

Griffith 200-5-030

photo courtesy of Griffith Car Club

Griffith Series 400-6-025

photo courtesy of Marshall Moore

Griffith Series 200-5-145

photo courtesy Walt Hotchkiss

200-6-001E wringing it out on the track

photo courtesy of Marshall Moore

Early TVR Jomar

photo courtesy of Griffith Car Club

200-5-191

photo courtesy of Joe Rauh

Joe Rauh's Series 400-5-009

photo courtesy of Griffith Car Club

200-5-160 running the pylons in an Autocross

photo courtesy of Griffith Car Club

200-5-179 cutting the lights at the drag strip

photo courtesy the Griffith Car Club

British Griffith 200-010

(Note the right hand drive and Series 400 body style)

photo courtesy of Griffith Club

British Griffith 200-003

photo courtesy of Intermeccanica/Reisner

Car designer, Frank Reisner in a Torino roadster

photo courtesy of Joe Rauh

Serious racing setup for 400-5-009

photo courtesy of Intermeccanica/Reisner

Frank Reisner's Apollo GT

photo courtesy C.J. LaFalce

Griffith Series 600-5-004

photo courtesy Bill Buan

Grifith Series 400-6-055

photo by Mike Mooney

George Potekhen passing a Sunbeam Tiger at Lime Rock in 200-5-168

photo courtesy of Griffith Car Club

Series 200-5-015

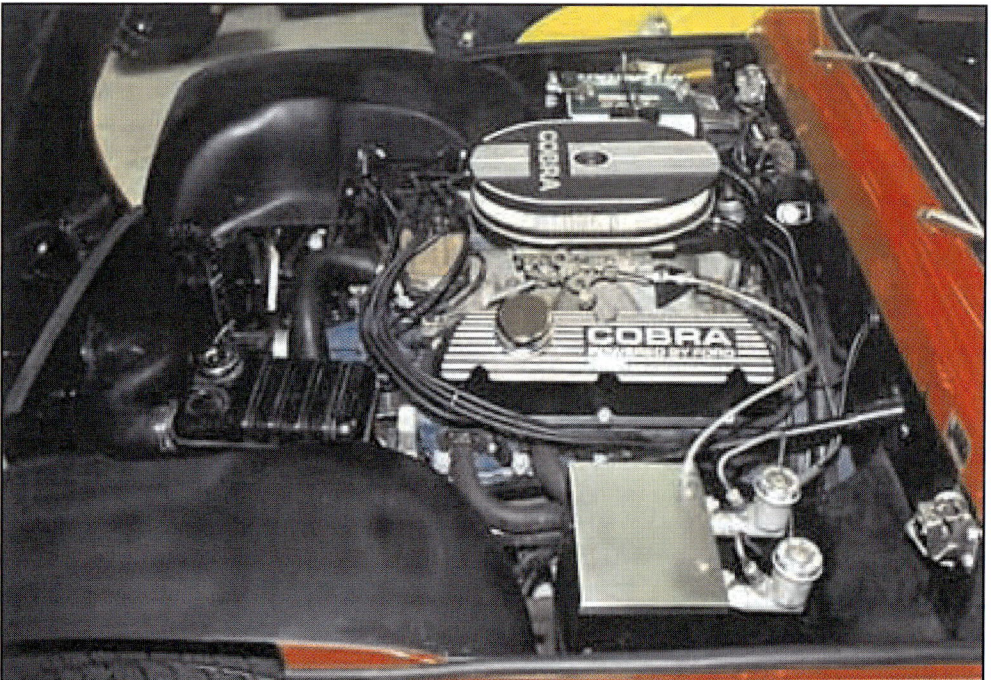

photo courtesy of Griffith Car Club

Engine Compartment of 200-5-063

six

Series 200

"..There is a time for departure even when there's no certain place to go."
Tennessee Williams

As can be attested to by any Griffith owner, none of these cars were without fault. From the start as the cars were being assembled at the Eileen Way factory the gremlins were showing up and giving no quarter.

During the interviews most of those who knew of the early history of the car indicated that the world introduction was at the New York Auto Show in April of 1964 yet there were some reports that it was first shown at the Boston Auto Show that same month.

That was not the matter of primary importance, though. What was significant is that the car chosen to represent the marque was probably one of the most unique in New York that year. Bob Bergen at Pioneer Auto Body on Long Island's North Shore was given the chore of producing a "plaid" car, one that was painted in the Griffith family tartan colors.

It sat in a section beside the Chrysler exhibit at the show and raised quite a few eyebrows, stirring the necessary enthusiasm for potential sales. It was reported that more than twenty serious customers signed up that weekend.

While the glitter of New York was sparkling in the eyes of the public, the assembly line at 141 Eileen Way in Syosset was awakening. One of the first problems out of the box involved the cooling system.

Factory representative checks out Griffith

The original Grantura III was fitted with a mild mannered little four cylinder that needed a mere wisp of cooling British breeze wafting through the small radiator to keep the engine coolant within limits.

Now the 289 cid engine that Jack decided to stuff under the bonnet produced a thermal rise that, coupled with the original equipment, was unable to keep up with the transfer of that good ol' Ford-produced heat. George Clark had seen this problem long before production started. Even the installation of an efficient and thermostatically-controlled cooling fan would just barely help with keeping the temperature within limits.

The Griffith Years

He had been adamant that an efficient Harrison radiator was put out front of the Ford engine and had requested that this become part of the factory standard. Had had one antagonist though. Dick Monnich had insisted that the original radiators were sufficient and that plant manager, Dick Triano, and George must work with it.

This decision would come back to haunt not only the post production run but not until later years, as future Griffith owners started to retro-fit the older units with newer and more efficient heat exchangers, would the problem finally be corrected.

To get the car ready to accept the Ford engine many changes had to be done. The chassis had to be widened about nine inches and the front suspension hangers were beefed up. The front cross tubes in the chassis were redesigned and strengthened.

Then the front cross tubes had to be moved forward about six inches to clear the deeper and larger Ford oil pan. At the rear end of the car, the BMC rear carrier was good enough for the four-banger that once occupied the engine compartment in the car but, as would be learned during the early days in production, was not able to stand up to the gaffe of the potent 289.

Shop manager, Dick Triano, designed the mounting location for the Jag rears when the production line ran into problems with the MGB units. The BMCs couldn't take any abuse, in fact, Len Bailey, one of the workers said that he broke one just taking it out for a "little test drive."

George Clark said that the rear end required stronger universal joints as well as new hub carriers, which changed the angle to accommodate larger tires and wheels since the Griffith uses larger rims. The drive shaft was a shortened Ford design.

The engine mounting location was moved four inches to the rear compared with the four-cylinder mill. As the engine bay was filled with more and more "stuff," the steering rack had to be offset in relation to the steering column which had to be moved to clear the left exhaust pipes from the 289.

Engine compartment awaiting installation of drive train

The first TVR bodies that Dick Monnich delivered to Eileen Way were three Grantura bodies sans engines. They were set up to orient the production line and to make the necessary adjustments in making it all come together before the stream of bodies would arrive from Hoo Hill in the U.K., the home of TVR.

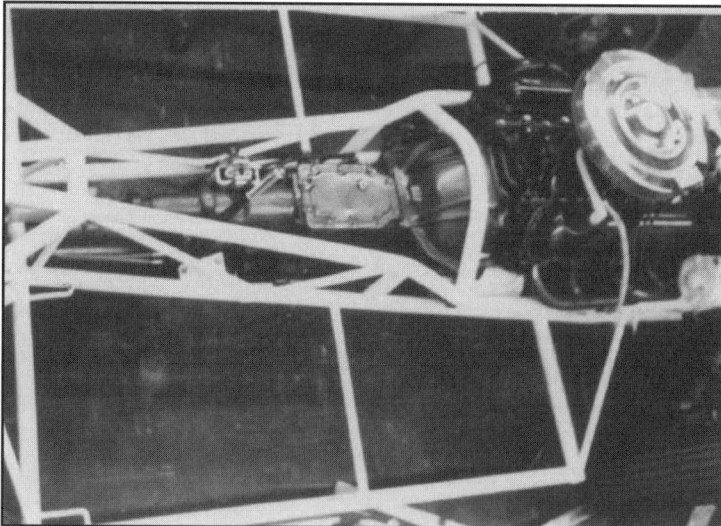

Engine and transmission installed in TVR-based chassis

The Griffith Years

As in the prototype the engines in these three cars were mounted lower in the chassis since the hood bubble, one of the prominent changes for the transition, had not yet been incorporated into the Grantura body. This bubble was necessary on the Griffith hoods to accommodate the taller carburetor and air cleaner.

These three cars, now known as serial numbers 015, 016 and 017, were an enigma in the research of the car. They were all equipped with the Grantura-style license plate frames, rear wing (fender) trim and other identifiable quirks. Each of the owners had no idea as to what separated these three cars from the rest except for the fact that they appeared to be early off the production line.

Even though these three cars sported the Grantura markings, they were not the only cars that wore the previous TVR trappings. For instance, 200-5-011, which is among some of the first draft cars delivered, still has the Grantura III trim and regalia since it was one of the first group of bodies delivered to Eileen Way. It seems that the factory was still sorting out and mixing some Grantura III bodies in with the Griffith order.

After the first three Grantura-bodied cars, were being readied for sale the factory in England was being stretched to the walls to produce the bodies in number and quality required for Griffith.

Within a few weeks six Griffith bodies were sent and these were followed by six more. The assembly line was getting up to speed.

When the first of the cars were getting ready for the road and the tanks filled with gasoline, it was found that most of the fuel tanks were pourous. The cars were shipped without any petrol for the required safety concerns but this presented another bump in the road to perfection. Dick Triano had to do something quick and now a new member of the team was about to lend a hand in getting rid of yet another delay in production.

Willie Seitz, who had met Bobby Brown, Jr. and Roger Teck at C.W. Post College, was again called on to solve another problem. Working after hours at his family's metal spinning machine shop in Freeport, Willie produced a fuel tank made from two halves of spun, lead-coated steel stock and soldered together to form a reliable gas tank.

This method of overcoming the leakage problem continued for about three months and production decided to try a new idea out. One of the first duties that Jim Ketcher, who joined the factory team in July of '64, had was to remove the tanks on all inbound bodies.

From there he would take them to a local radiator shop to have them resoldered and tested prior to having any gasoline being introduced. Jim related that later in the production year that the radiator shop no longer welcomed the job and turned down the work. Rumor has it that the radiator shop felt that it wasn't worth the time and the aggravation, or maybe the factory started to get the word.

The cars would now sport a new "fix" for the leaky fuel reservoirs. Someone decided that a quick and easy repair could be done by wrapping the tank seam in fiberglass mat and resin to contain the fuel. I'm sure that with the regulations that are in force today, that another Ralph Nader would surface proclaiming the unroadworthiness of the beast.

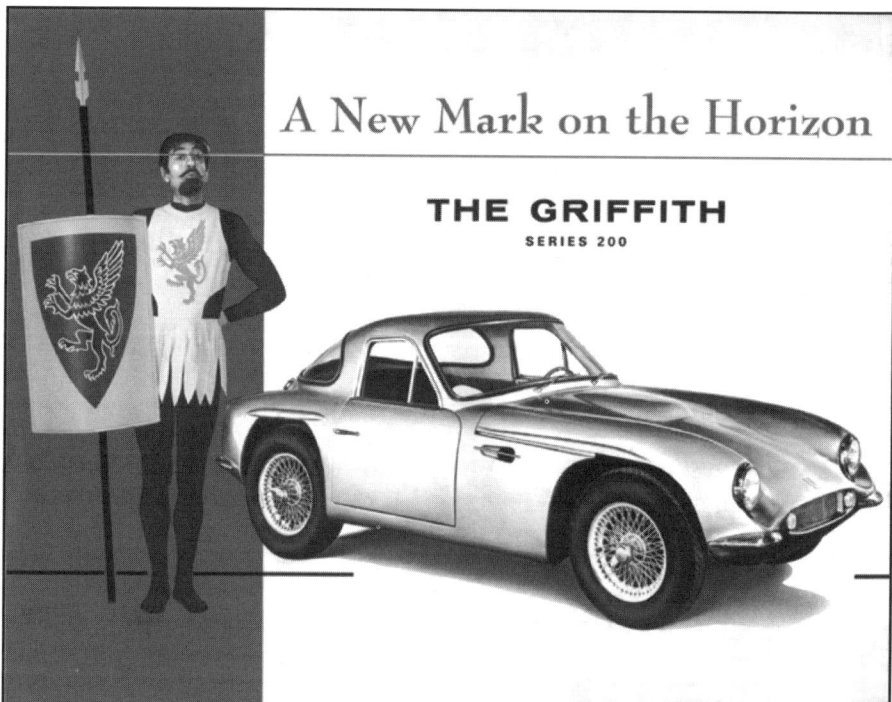

courtesy Jack Griffith collection

Cover of first Griffith Series 200 sales brochure

The Griffith Years

With the production line humming along, Jim Ketcher was also assigned to taking each car as it left the final build stage and do a quick test drive in preparing the car for its new owner. In the meantime as one problem was dealt with another problem usually popped up.

Since the car was mostly built for a four cylinder engine in England, some of the driveline components did not require all too much heft. But now, as Roger Teck put it, "Whenever you slammed the gas pedal to the floor, everything behind the transmission would break." Jim would learn the hard way.

Mainly, the bolts connecting the half-shafts between the differential and the hub carriers were ungraded mild steel. Jim's duties now included removal of all of these bolts and replacing them with graded and more reliable case-hardened bolts.

As the first of the engine and transmission units arrived at Eileen Way, the assembly crew found that those equipped with the 55 ampere/hour alternators were posing another glitch. The location of the alternator was interfering with the installation of the engine so the alternators were removed and replaced with easily-available 30 a/h generators. That fit well but looks ain't everything!

Many owners would find that the art of judicial electrical usage of appliances would become necessary if they wanted to finish the trip that they started.

In the design of the TVR steering geometry a situation arose that was not experienced in its original trim, that of being launched with a smallish 4-cylinder engine.

When the Griffith was fed the coals, the front end would lift and a severe case of "bump steer" was dumped into the drivers now-busy hands. Both front tires wanted to go their separate ways. What was needed to correct this cross-eyed problem was just about impossible at that time to retrofit to the car. Willie Seitz said that the only way that they could temporarily fix it was to lower the front of the car which only partly solved the problem.

Another setback on the production schedule was that as the cars were being sent out a few would have to have their differentials modified with aftermarket changes. Some opted to have either a Jaguar or an occasional Corvette independent suspension rear installed.

photo courtesy of Hayes Harris

Griffith Series 200-5-123

But, in a flash of wisdom gone awry, someone at the factory probably figured that a quick fix to prevent any returns or warranty work was to drain the 90-W gear oil out of the differential and replace it with a heavier-weight and gooey STP oil additive. There are no records nor recollections as to what resulted from this "repair" but it apparently went unnoticed by the customer.

Engineering wanted a shorter steering rack to reduce the serious amount of correction needed to hold this beast going straight but the manufacturer and its stateside sales representative would prevail. The longer rack would stay and so would the bump steer. It's something that the "...Emptor would have to Caveat."

As more and more Griffiths were produced one more weakness was beginning to show up on the "list." One such car, VIN 200-4-119, purchased by Paul Plummer, and was immediately shipped to Willie Seitz's shop in Smithtown, New York.

The Griffith Years

Editor's note: At the present time there are two registered Griffiths with the VIN of 200-5-119 and both can trace their origin to the factory. In researching the problem, the Griffith Registry has determined that one is most likely 200-5-118 since there is no #118 in the registry and that the very thin foil VIN plate that the factory attached to the firewall could have been poorly stamped with the "8" appearing as a "9" but the investigation continues.

Seizing the moment in high performance history and bowing to the demand for faster and faster cars, Willie Seitz and George Clark had decided to go into business building engines and doing head work for street and track applications. The partnership, named W.E.S. Engineering, was nestled away in a small garage complex on New York State Rt. 25 (Jericho Turnpike) in Smithtown. This duo had gained the reputation of being able to massage some serious horsepower out of the Detroit iron and word was spreading quickly.

Willie had done his apprenticeship at the shop of Bill Frick, the birthplace of the famed Studillac and Fordillac cars. Frick would be one of the forerunners of the hybrid Euro/American school of speciality cars.

Editor's note: How many who are reading this book remember the Studillac? How about the Fordillacs? Well they were stock new cars with the tiny modification, a Cadillac engine, and they went like hell!

Bill Frick was a major figure in hot rod and racing circles in the 1950's. This custom-built car was designed by Michelotti, and sported a hand-made body by Vignale, a modified Studebaker chassis, Studebaker front suspension, a modified 1955 Cadillac Eldorado V-8, four speed manual transmission, and Mercury differential. Evidently the car was not completed until 1957.

Three Bill Frick Specials were made: a prototype coupe, a convertible, and this coupe FREDERICK J. ROTH

1957 Bill Frick Special

photos courtesy of Frederick J. Roth

Plummer had wanted to add **the** fastest Griffith to his modest automobile collection and George and Willie would be called on to do the trick. After adding the after market items that would guarantee its place on the totem pole, the British differential unit had to be replaced. At that time it was a choice of installing a Corvette or a Jaguar rear and in this case it was the Corvette unit.

This car could easily stand on it rear tires at the slightest nudge of the accelerator. It had to be judiciously coaxed out of the hole when the coefficient of friction was at its peak in order to prevent an unexpected and thought-provoking launch.

Several Griffiths were given similar treatment at the W.E.S. shop and the reputation of the little Ford-powered car was spreading quickly. One such owner would hang out with one of the numerous "run what you brung" crowds and after a couple of hole shots, it was soon never able to find any more "friendly" competition on the street.

As the number of 200s delivered grew, the new body style model was not only being built but was introduced to the public. In short order the newer Manx-tailed version of the Grantura had been released from the molds and enroute to Plainview, NY.

After Jim Ketcher was finished prepping each of the cars for delivery as they rolled off the assembly line it required an occasional trip around the "back forty." Since he was the most likely to have the keys, Jim was probably the first driver of just about all of the cars.

Once in a while, though, some of the workers would try them out just for the fun of it. One particular team member, Joey DeTore, who had a penchant inadvertantly disassembling things that were totally assembled, liked to take advantage of the company perk.

In the midst of the few forays that Joey had with the mighty, yet unforgiving, Griffith, he managed to; A) back a Griffith into and through a fence on the Long Island Expressway service road while he was drag racing with another Griff doing some nasty damage to the car; B) put a forklift completely through the brick wall at the factory; and, C) crack the frame of a Griffith when he launched it in a high-speed encounter with a raised railroad crossing.

A few years later a similar situation happened to Charlie Terhune when he bought a Griffith, chassis number 200-5-119, (the other one) from a fellow in Texas who was the second owner of the car. The details, though, differed a bit.

The original owner had used the Griff as a daily driver in the Chicago area and it seemed logical when the new owner decided to drive the car to Texas. As he was nearing his home just a few miles from his destination in the Lone Star State, he crossed a set of railroad tracks and the car CLUNKED and everything just sat down and started to scrape.

As many TVR and Griffith owners have learned, often too late, a major design flaw showed up. As the cars were built the chassis tubes were connected to the body with fiberglass wrapping. What would then happen was the rest of the story.

With accumulated moisture inside the steel frame tubes they rusted inside the fiberglass wrapping weakening the chassis and eventually breaking.

Charlie bought the car after it had sat out in the Texas sun and had several parts canabalized from it over a few years intending to restore it. But there it sat and then put on the block, purchased twice more and is now nearing restoration by its new owner, Dave Jencson.

The Griffith Years

Editor's note: The historians who covered the automotive scene often tended to slight the Griffith in the pages of the magazines of the era so that many figures and facts surrounding this car were almost lost. I say, "almost" because with the help of many of the people who worked on the cars, these stories were recalled, verified and preserved.

According to Len Bailey, not all of the Series 200 Griffiths that came off the line were equipped with a four-barrel carburetor. Nearly half of them were fitted with a two-barrel and then many owners switched to the larger intakes. The reported difference between the two versions was about 30 horsepower and Len would sometimes help to tweak a bit more of that horsepower out of the engines for the customers.

Shop manager Dick Triano had looked over the assembled talent in the shop and would often pick the ones who were stronger in a particular area and run with his abilities. One of those workers was not only was an integral part of the assembly team but also drove in some serious SCCA weekend racing. Len Bailey had already made a name for himself piloting his Jaguar XK-120 in competition and eventually winning the series championship national title in that car.

Len would serve Dick well also as a test driver who could translate from real time experience to sorting out the handling quirks of the Griffith and constantly trying to improve the breed.

While the series 200 was in production several in-house modifications had to be made to make a more workable finished product. One of those implemented was an improved hydraulic clutch slave cylinder mounting bracket. Len, along with Dick Triano, had devised an improved design to do the job.

The bracket design model was given to Willie Seitz who machined the mold and cast the fixture in his machine shop. It was eventually incorporated into the production cars and some even were retro-fitted.

The Griffith Years

With a total of about eight men on the production line the series 200 cars were coming off the line at the rate of as many as twenty cars per week. The reality of the series 400 was on the table and bodies were already being delivered.

Until early in 1965 all of the Griffiths built were being sold in the United States but that soon changed. That was until the 1965 Racing Car Show in the U.K. at Olympia in January of that year the car was now available in "right hand drive" trim in the U.K. and priced at £1,342 in basic trim and £1,620 equipped.

Oddly, this was immediately following the beginning of the dock strike hampering delivery of the Griffith bodies to New York.

Griffiths lined up for assembly

The 271 hp version was priced at £1,488 and £1797 respectively. Possibly the only variant in this equation was that the earliest Griffith possibly registered there was a TVR with the British-based serial number of BFR400B and was being readied for production. This car was originally registered on the 23 October 1964 as a pale blue TVR Griffith 200, with the owner of record being listed as Grantura Engineering Ltd. at Hoo Hill.

The Griffith Years

Although registered as a Griffith 200, BFR400B was in fact the development car for the Manx-tailed Griffith 400. Stan Kilcoyne was working for Grantura Engineering at the time and he believes that the car was built during the spring of 1964 just following the stateside introduction of the Series 200.

photo courtesy of Colin Archibald

British Griffith Series 400 BFR400B

In comparison with the series 200, the fiberglass at the rear of this car is much thicker than normal production cars and one theory that rattles about is that this car was used as a buck to make the Manx-tail molds for the production cars. BFR400B is currently owned by Colin Archibald.

The cat was now out of the bag. The motoring media had already presented a few "spy" shots of the new model 400 in sparse publications and Jack was ready to show the new and improved version of his dream.

The Griffith Years

94

seven

Series 400

"..There are moments when everything goes well; don't be frightened, it won't last."
                                                            Jules Renard

The previous design of the Grantura III-based Griffith made enough noise in the sports car market to warrant some notice in the motoring press. Some irresponsible publications even did product and driving reports on the Griffith without having ever gotten to within fifty feet of one and yet other writers were doing what what they were paid to do; writing the truth.

Sometimes that would not come across in the best interests of the factory since no matter when the interview was done, the Griffith organization would sometimes appear to be two completely different companies depending who spoke or when they were interviewed.

One writer, reporting on the size of the storage area, said that "…you can squeeze in a soft bag, a very small suitcase and a couple of toothbrushes…" in the stowage area behind the seat. "Maybe a container of dental floss as well" he went on.

The Griffith Years

The most significant departure in model structure was the new Manx-tail and larger rear glass along with other design changes that separated it from the 200. From first blush the 200 was overshadowed by the 400 just in the "looks" department alone and it was apparent that the improvements would insure that the car was guaranteed to be a success.

Walter Wurzbach, a seriously infected British car driver who served our country well in the United States Air Force, had the foresight to see the Griffith Series 400 for what it really was; a winner.

As a pilot for Uncle Sam. Walt was stationed in various locations around the globe and had the opportunity to drive and test both the ridiculous and the sublime.

On the 3rd of September of 1965 he strode into a place named **Parkway Service Center** on South Eglin Parkway in Fort Walton Beach, Florida, plunked his cash on the counter and bought a Griffith 400, with the VIN of 400-5-052. The sales ticket was one not unlike one that you'd get at a dry cleaner shop.

The receipt noted that he had traded in a 1960 Sprite and he had paid a hefty bottom line of $5,469.20 for the car. Considering that a well-equipped high performance Mustang that same year was listing in at about $3,500, this was in Corvette or Cobra territory… but Walt wanted a Cobra Killer!

Over the ensuing years Walt drove and raced his Griffith and very successfully. When he was transferred to Germany he travelled extensively on the continent and had fun with the car, which, by the way, he still owns. He got involved with the local and regional sports car clubs and went racing.

His efforts behind the wheel earned him a few titles as he mowed his way through England and the continent and it was not only in the Griffith that he made a name for himself. He was twisting the steering wheel of a Formula Ford on the tracks and burning up the roads with his hot little Grif'.

But Walt is not the story here. It's the Griffith 400. As something broke or needed an upgrading, Walt made the change or replaced the part. Walt did what just about every Griffith owner since 1963 when the first car was built has done; improved the breed.

photo courtesy of Walt Wurzbach

Walt Wurzbach's Series 400 # 052

It never had anyone take the time to bring to forefront the needs of taking this light little fiberglass sports car that was built to accept a four cylinder engine and be overstressed with an overpowered engine and driveline that might have added a mere 75 or so pounds of weight to its total.

History repeats itself too often and it did in the 400. Some of the needed upgrades for problems that plagued the 200 were corrected. The engine was listed in the promo literature as the 225 hp version of the venerable 289 and the option as the 271 hp Cobra powerplant.

One observation made by the man who was doing the lion's share of the "first drives" for the car, Jim Ketcher, was that the 200 would pull the 400 out of the hole owing to the difference in the gearing between the two models.

The 200 was fitted with the low performance version of the engine and it carried as part of the package the wide ratio "top loader" transmission with a

2.72:1 first gear. The differential, the original BMC, had a 4.11:1 ratio providing a launch torque multiplication of just a tick over 11:1.

photo courtest Hayes Harris

Griffith series 440-5-054

Now to look at this in perspective, the high performance option was given a close-ratio gearbox from the factory attached to the rear of the bell housing. The theory for this was that if a high performance car has a narrower power arc in the torque and horsepower curve then the gear changes should permit the car to lose fewer RPMs between shifts and thereby transmitting more power to the rear wheels without going into the low-torque and low horsepower ranges of the cam.

Put into more civilized terms, the close ratio box would give a smoother transition between gears without forcing the engine to encroach into the lower powered segments of its regime while accelerating through the gears.

Now pick up your slide rules and figure this out. The newer Griffiths came equipped with a stronger rear but with a more anemic and higher geared differential, a 2.73:1 ratio. The close ratio box was blessed with a 2.32:1 gearing.

So multiply that by the rear gearing and you come up with a weak-kneed 6.33:1 launch figure.

So here we have the 200 with a low end torque strength and a launch multiplication of 11.18:1 against the 400 equipped with gobs of top-end horsepower coming out of the hole with a 6.33:1 rubber band and who's going to get to the 200 yard maker first? That's a no brainer. The 200 has it hands down while the 400 is burning up the clutch looking for a great torque curve.

As soon as the competition found out that the new and improved 400 was out for fresh meat they all tried playing catch-up, but the 400 was hard to catch. The Achilles Heel in the equation turned out not to be another car but something that neither Jack Griffith nor Mark Donohue could overcome; a dock strike.

The Series 400 was introduced to the public on November of 1964. After so many of the 200s were produced and the media were having fun either writing or lying about it the 400 was on their doorsteps waiting for a shot at the prize.

The best current records indicate that the last produced 200 was given the number of about 190 with a few question marks in and around the mix. Production run figures show that the Series 400 topped off at 59 before the dock strike took its toll and then eventually there were ten Series 600 cars built.

In a May, 1966 magazine interview Jack Griffith was asked the final production number over the three model run and he indicated that about 265 were built. This was probably closer to the truth that the projected numbers that were bragged about just as production started. At one time the projection was that 750 cars would be sold out before the end of the first summer of 1964.

The 400 was cut off at the knees with the dock strike. No TVR bodies would be arriving at the loading dock and Jack was in the middle of introducing the 600. There was nothing that he could hope for short of a miracle to salvage the wreck.

The Griffith Years

TVR/Grantura Engineering, struggling through the effects that the dock strike dealt and, after gasping its last breath went into receivership. Once again the TVR organization was running on empty. While Jack Griffith was trying to come to terms with the doubt of the future of the Griffith Car corporation, Grantura fell to its financial knees in August of 1965 keying the entry of Arthur and Martin Lilley. TVR Engineering Ltd. was the "phoenix" that rose out of the ashes, at least on that side of the pond.

Someone decided that with all of these bodies piling up on the TVR property that the momentum shouldn't stop there. The idea for the British Griffith was born and the chassis numbering system continued with a slight change from the USA numbering system, but in January of 1967 the decision was made to remove the Griffith nameplate.

The outgrowth from the British Griffiths was given the name of Tuscan by Martin Lilley in an unsuccessful attempt to quelch the Griffith failure. The serial numbers immediately following the last British Griffith number of 200-010 and the first Tuscan took on the VIN of 200-011.

The standard Tuscans were treated to higher quality fittings and a premium polished wooden dash panel and fitted with the 195 bhp 289 engine but another model would sport the letters SE following the name if it were fitted with the High Performance 289/271 bhp engine.

This transition eventually became the foundation on which TVR would base its new image of V-8 power in the fiberglass body. This all due to the foresight that began in Jack Griffith's Ford dealership.

But now back in the States it was time for Jack to salvage the dominoes that were falling.

The Griffith Years

eight

Series 600

"..If you live long enough, you'll see that every victory turns into defeat."
Simone de Beauvoir 1908 - 1986

Contracts were already in place for the production of the Series 600 and nothing could be delivered, save the first ten bodies that were sitting there, idling at the Old Country Road factory.

It was a thoroughly different design. Instead of staying with the TVR/fiberglass body, Jack had decided to go to an offshore design and production sources to build the new car. He knew that the TVR/Ford marriage would not last and he also wanted to present a distinctive and fresh design to the motoring world.

Engaging the talents of Bob Cumberford, a former General Motors designer and John Crosthwaite, a British chassis, Jack signed on with Hungarian-born Canadian, Frank Reisner, owner of **Carrozzeria Intermeccanica** of Turin, a small, low-volume auto manufacturing firm in Italy to hammer out the new steel body and mount it on Reisner's steel frame.

The Griffith Years

John Crosthwaite was a Britisher with design experience both in Europe and the States with chassis design and fabrication experience working on cars from Lotus, Cooper Dolphin of San Diego, Mickey Thompson and B.R.M. His responsibility included the review and correction to Frank Reisner's chassis and suspension design for the new Griffith, while Cumberford did the body shape and also worked out the general concept and proportion of the car.

photo courtesy Jack Griffith collection
Apollo GT with Griffith display at 1965 New York Auto Show

Frank's first hybrid car a few years back was a Buick-powered coupe called the Apollo GT. After about ninety cars were produced Franco Scaglione was said to have developed the follow-up design that would eventually transform into the Series 600 likeness.

Reisner's firm had begun life as North-East Engineering, producing speed equipment, some Peugeot-based Formula junior cars and a little GT coupe fitted with the Steyr engine for sale in Austria. He later had switched exclusively to body construction, and for the Apollo he had produced some quality bodies of excellent fit and design. This was just what the doctor ordered for Jack Griffith. In

April, 1965, he arranged to purchase several chassis and body units for the Series 600 Griffith from Reisner's Intermeccanica.

photo courtesy of Jack Griffith collection

Griffith Series 600 at 1965 New York Auto Show

Jack had envisioned delivering about 2,000 of these cars each year but the rattling at the Griffith factory started to quiet as news drifted in that TVR Grantura had shut down after posting a five-figure loss for the previous year. This blow to the supply line left nearly a half-year's gap in production between the 400 and 600.

The final design of the series 600 was eye-appealing and crisp, and in retrospect, far ahead of its time. Reisner farmed out the work for the manufacture of the car components to several sub-contractors and the first few cars were built and air-lifted to New York. The dock strike was taking a heavy toll, not only on Griffith, but also on the economic life of the Eastern United States.

The Griffith Years

Ford was supplying engine and transmission assemblies to Griffith but the cash that it required to keep that supply line open was failing rapidly. Attempts were made to cover the costs but bills had to be paid and another domino fell.

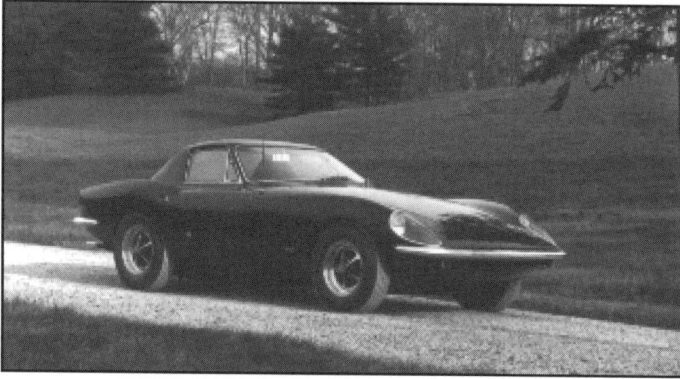

Intermeccanica Griffith Series 600

When Griffith was informed that Ford would be pulling all the engine assemblies out of the shop at Old Country Road he jumped on the next "red-eye" for Detroit to line up the next generation engine/transmission for his new car.

Griffith got on the phone and immediately contacted his old friends at Chrysler Corporation. After opening the corporate doors he brought one of the Series 600s to Chrysler and met with Buck Rogers, the engineer who was repsonsible for the original Chrysler "300" project. After negotiating a deal he succeeded in getting a raft of 273 cubic inch displacment engines delivered to the Griffith factory. Eight were backed up with four-speed manual transmissions and two had the Mopar torqueflite automatics.

Since the Series 600 was built and engineered for the relatively lightweight Ford 289 cid engine this would present a unique opportunity for Mark Donohue, who was heading up the engineering department at Griffith. After his engineering crew scurried about to change the motor mounts and under-the-bonnet accessories Mark had to reset the figures. They had to try to accommodate this relatively light car, weighing in at about 2300 pounds wet, to accept a lower-powered, physically-larger and heavier driveline.

273-CUBIC INCH HIGH-PERFORMANCE V-8 ENGINE

File photograph

"It might take four months to get the bugs our of the car with the staff and resources we have available now," Mark said later that year to **Brock Yates** in an interview for **Car and Driver** magazine.

Not only did the new car suffer badly from severe understeer, but with the additional weight on the front end, braking was a nightmare. Brake line pressure was completely out of balance, spring rates made the front end want to become friendly with the pavement and handling characteristics were terribly discouraging. This resulted in a nightmare of mismatched combinations which helped to doom the new Griffith.

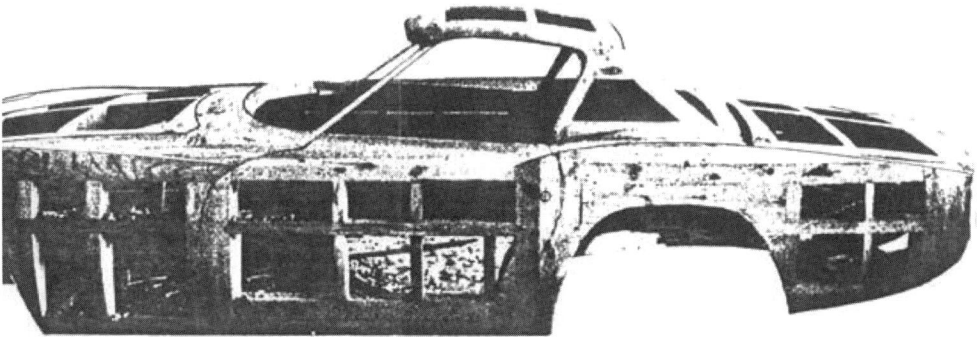

photo by Intermeccanica/courtesy Jack Griffith collection

Griffith Series 600 body buck

The Griffith Years

They had found the slippery slope in the decline of the Griffith history. Jack was understanding that it was time to try to keep his head above water and the factory building at Old Country Road was an expense that had to be released. There were no cars being produced and those that were in house were being pieced together to sell to the public. Anything and everything that was in the building was for sale.

One of the items in the "garage sale" was a factory "mule," a car that had been used for the past two years as a test bed, one of the first Griffiths assembled. It was eventually branded with serial number 001E (Experimental), cleaned up and ended up being sold as a new Griffith in 1966.

photo by Mike Mooney

Griffith Series 22 #001E

After going through a few owners, the Griffith that owns serial number 200-6-001E eventually found its way to a home in Homestead, Florida.

For one long, long year, Griffith tried to keep the company going as the financial walls were crumbling around him. The crippling dock strike had finally gone away but the damaging results were still haunting many businesses, Griffith among them.

The Griffith Years

The plant in Plainview had become deserted except for Jack, a few leftovers from the formerly-busy work crew and about ten Griffith Series 600s. Still clinging to the hopes that the new body and its re-engineered powerplant would get legs and find a market to take advantage of the former momentum that the car had generated, but it was not to be.

Mark Donohue had been busy working on many of the design problems that the Reisner chassis and car had presented. The test driving chores had indicated that the overweight Plymouth 273 inch engine was not good. The entire car was still yearning for the light Ford 289 that it had been designed to surround and this would be only the tip of the troubled iceberg.

Every way that the design was skewed and the suspension tweaked it always went back to the fact that the car would have to be completely rebuilt around the engine and transmission. Of the ten 600s sitting in the shop, the first one, which sported a brilliant yellow paint job, was fitted with one of the two fitted with the TorqueFlite transmission, the remaining with four-speeds.

No matter what was done with the suspension or brakes, the test drives always resulted in too many head-shaking trips to the drawing board and not enough solutions to the increasing problems that were festering.

In the midst of all of this, Jack had taken in a partner/buyer. Chuck Petri, a businessman from Manhasset, Long Island, New York, who had wanted to become a part of automotive history, would eventually buy the company from Jack, who would then stay on as an advisor during the transition. When the papers were signed for the transfer of ownership, it was Mark Donohue's signature that would appear on the "witness" line of the document.

In early of '66, Jack made a last stab at promotion of the car. When **Car and Driver** magazine sent the venerable and seasoned reporter **Brock Yates** to size up the situation, the resultant story branded with a headline that screamed **"GRIFFITH: MAN AND MACHINE IN A SILENT WORKSHOP,"** it painted a editorial picture of the company in its death throes.

The Griffith Years

The lead-in photo was a shot of Jack looking forlorn with six cars festering in the shop behind him and a lone worker walking among the automotive clutter. Jack later would describe that picture as "..the worst picture of me, ever!"

Jack Griffith in the "Silent Workshop"

With what was probably the last gasp of breath for the Griffith and the company, the bells were ringing but Jack didn't want to hear them.

Gathering up a skeleton crew of just about six workers, Jack took a seasonal lease on a building in the east end town of Bridgehampton on Long Island's south fork in April of 1966. With a few last helpers, the shop and its remaining pieces of equipment were moved into its last home.

Hoping to capitalize on the upcoming race season at the "Bridge" and to possibly secure some much needed backing, the Griffith organization was slowly zippering itself into a cocoon of anonymity. By November of that year when the seasonal lease was history, so was the company.

What now stands as a food market on the west end of town witnessed the dying throbs of life of the Griffith organization; an attempt to marry the lightweight European sports car body with the lightweight American V-8 engine.

Steve Wilder, a former writer for Joe Lane, Griffith's ad agency, and Bob Cumberford, the co-designer of the 600 body, would be waiting in the wings watching as the cadaver was cooling off. But Jack still had a few yards of fight in him.

He slowly sold off the remaining models to whomever would come up with the cash and by the end of the summer season of 1966, in the glitzy and star-studded Hamptons on the East End of Long Island, the doors were closed on this segment of automotive history. The obituary of the Griffith Motor Corporation was set in stone.

The Griffith Years

nine

The Players

"..For many men that stumble at the threshold are well foretold that danger lurks within."
William Shakespeare

The story and history of the Griffith motorcar brought many thoughts to mind. Was it the car that brought the people together or was it the opposite? Did the car become the giant magnet drawing the talent into a ball of creativity waiting for the "thousand monkeys" idea to play out?

The obvious conclusion was to put the list of the players together and let you, the reader, make the judgement. In the twelve years that we spent chasing down the workers who were involved from date of conception through gestation and throughout the turmoil-ridden life of the car we learned that the common thread was the love of motoring.

The kinship that swept through this curious and talented group of tradesmiths that were assembled for this project was the ultimate challenge of playing midwife to a brutally fast and ill-handling car topping the list. Home life systematically trotted in near the back of the pack.

Some were products of the early days of post-WWII racing and they brought the appetizer to the table. They had the experience that was necessary for a strong foundation for the rest of the cast.

Then the entrée was served by the magicians who had been doing their journeyman chores at the altars of these wise high priests of the sport. The apprentices wanted to learn. They thirsted for the knowledge that would qualify them one day as masters in the engineering and automotive field and were willing to do the chores required to learn their craft.

Jack Griffith – With a story that is well documented in the early pages of this book, his first love was promotion of an idea. Any idea that would change things. Things that were fast, hot and sexy. Things that had loud and throaty

exhaust pipes, noisy lifters and big tires. Y'know, hot rods and fast cars.

Armed with an idea that reeked of "all of the above," Jack would gather his team and open their minds with his electric imagination to put his "idea" on paper and then eventually into production.

It worked for Jack before the Griffith and it has worked since then. He was, is and will continue to be indefatigable.

Lew Schulz – The first time that you would have the opportunity to meet Lew you would find a gentle man who would never raise his voice in anger or criticize in a negative tone of voice. It was this ability that would help him to recognize Mark Donohue's latent talent of and forging him into the winner that he became.

When confronted with any particular situation that needed correction Lew would respond to it as being, not as a problem, but as an opportunity; an opportunity to improve on and polish and make it shine as an accomplishment to put on your trophy shelf.

A view of Lew Schulz that not too many people would see was that he was an extremely calculating driver. Though he never competed in any long term motoring competition theater Lew could handle any vehicle into which he would fit his large frame. Just trying to follow him from point "A" to point "B" in the family station wagon would cause the following driver to never leave view of the rear end of Lew's car because to do so would certainly mean that he'd lose you without even looking in the mirror.

After he left his foreign car dealership in the hands of the new owner, he and his wife had taken off on a three-month trip around the States to clear out the cobwebs. On his return he stepped into the shoes of sales manager at Griffith and performed his chores with the same energy that was his trademark.

When Lew left us a couple of years ago, his absence would leave some long term memories that will be hard to erase.

Mark Donohue – The story of Mark's life is written on the race tracks of the world. When he first sat behind the wheel of his new 1957 Corvette he reckoned that it was just a fast and cool chick magnet that went faster than any of the British "tin" that his college classmates were driving.

His future, though all too short, was predisposed by that moment in time and Mark went on to shatter records and win races in more racing venues and arenas than just about anyone else who ever turned a wheel. Mark had the knack of being able to turn a docile and inconsequential sports or sporty car into a winner, and all the while making it look easy.

In his book, **"The Unfair Advantage"** recently reprinted by his sons, David and Michael, Mark gave us all the benefit of being able to look into his soul and through his eyes as he rose through the ranks of national and international competition.

In this writer's own experience with Mark, I will never forget his easy way of getting an idea across to whomever he connected with and the structured and calculating manner with which he moved foreward. He would reflect seriously on a situation but he would **never** look back.

Whenever I tried to translate a situation that was encountered either within the front office of any of the Griffiths that I drove for him or some foolish idea for a design change, he would always say my name or call me "Matey," as he would do to many of us on the team, and approach the situation with a deep and simply-stated answer or ask one leading question that would unlock the door to the solution.

Mark was a friend who knew how to drive a car into regimes where it often was never designed to go, or if it were, he would take it deeper and cleaner to the extreme edges exploring the corners of its design envelope.

Richard "Dick" Monnich – Dick was someone who had the talent to formulate or run with an idea so that it could be a bit more marketable or workable to fit a broader spectrum of interest.

When Dick got hooked up with the Griffith machine he had a vision of helping to launch Jack Griffith into national prominence within the low-volume, speciality automotive manufacturing fraternity.

As many of the people who worked along with Dick would learn, he'd reportedly often hold the cards just a bit too close to the vest and would tend to keep them there hoping that the kitty would come his way. It would be a trait that would, in the end, work to his, and the company's disadvantage.

Given another place and another time, and armed with a slightly more positive outlook for a result-oriented achievement, Dick would have emerged a winner.

Dick Triano – As shop manager at Griffith, Dick had his hands full. He had to make sure that the cars were brought in all in one piece, prepped for assembly, VIN tags affixed, engine/transmission assemblies in place and wired, production line corrections made, line workers were where they belonged and were doing what they were assigned to do, certificates of origin were affixed to each car, and all cars leaving the factory were customer prepped.

Other than that, it was a pretty boring job. For a man who drove a rear-engined Chevrolet Corvair, which at that time was one of the more controversial and radical concept cars that the General brought to the public, it worked well for him to become the manager for a radical and controversial auto manufacturer. Dick's brother raced an Alfa Romeo in competition so it ran in the blood.

Whenever any fabrications at the Griffith plant were to be made, Dick would work with the design and engineering people to make sure that the "fix" could be done within budget and that if it were feasible, the new piece would work with the rest of the car.

Actually, Dick did this in a very professional manner and all this with his very eclectic and unusual crew of factory workers. Often he would call on an outside contractor, acutally someone who could be counted on to understand what was needed and was actually able to provide the service or part quickly.

He was one of the biggest cogs in this small wheel and, though unavailable for interview, was much on the minds and tongues of several of the people who helped in bringing their stories to the forefront.

The Griffith Years

Roger Teck – For the guy who was there when Jack needed the Sprint project formulated, Jack couldn't have picked a more qualified recruit. Roger had the credentials and the experience to make the idea work. A quiet student of physics, Teck had cut his teeth on the drag strip with his 1960 Corvette that was loaded with neat racing stuff out of the junk bin at the Bill Frick shop where he worked.

His leadership prowess led him to the position of president of the Oceanside Hot Rod Club, one of the early "drag and drive" clubs on Long Island, and also got him enough notoriety within the motoring fraternity in the area to be noticed. This was followed with a six-month hitch in the U.S. Navy Reserves.

Roger was originally hired by Jack Griffith to wrench the racing Cobra bridging the Bobby Brown, Jr – Mark Donohue era by about a month. After bringing George Clark on board to work on the Cobra, he was then put on the payroll to build the Griffith Sprint car for Jack.

When the TVR/Griffith project came to hatch, Roger was edged out when Dick Monnich dropped him in favor of George Clark, a more energetic character which, at the time, appealed to Monnich and his new venture.

Life after Griffith took him to work as a Lincoln-Mercury dealer parts manager and on to a boat yard in East Rockaway. IBM then took a chance and hired Roger as a customer engineer, a test engineer, a systems engineer in marketing and then into the planning department prior to retiring in the early Nineties.

Today, Roger spends his time flying and rebuilding old aircraft and also teaching the art of flight in the Northeast part of the country. Who knows what would have been the outcome of the Griffith had Roger been sanctioned to assign his calculating mind to the task?

George Clark – He wrenched for Mark Donohue, built the prototype Griffith and became the hinge pin on which Jack Griffith relied to start the momentum of seeing the concept come to fruition. That's all… or was it?

When George Clark moved into the catbird seat at Griffith Ford being handed the baton from Roger Teck, he relied on the street-level experience and knowledge that he had gained as a young upstart on the streets of Long Island, an area long-known as the breeding place of many of the early hot rodders.

At first it might have crossed the minds of the more seasoned people involved in the project, that this relatively, wet-behind-the-ears, defiant mechanic could put both of Jack Griffith's cars on stage and on schedule, but George did just that.

What enamored Dick Monnich to choose George over Roger Teck to fabricate the Griffith prototype eventually became the traits that drove a spike between them later on down the road. George's spontaniety and, as Mark Donohue would say, his "arrogance" in trying to make the car work, often over the objections of Monnich's immovable resolve, became the fork in the road.

The first-hand experience in making the Griffith Cobra handle and run strong for Mark Donohue was one of the best proving grounds for the virtual Griffith.

George was using the time spent with Mark and the Cobra to try to find the solutions for this TVR Grantura III that was being injected with Ford-powered steroids.

There are some who said that the teamwork and friendship that existed between George and Mark was a good part of the magic that sold Roger Penske on taking Donohue into the fold, but when Mark travelled into the thinning air of world-class auto racing George wouldn't be part of the deal.

The Griffith Years

Mark was still working in the Griffith organization trying to work out the problems with the Series 600 in early of 1966 and needed to have George back aboard for assistance.

After George was contacted, he said that he would return on one condition; that Dick Monnich would not be there if he were to come back to work at Griffith. The day before George came back, Monnich was gone. It was then that he would become part of the team, now down to about three in number, who would make the final move to the Hamptons on the east end of Long Island. The Series 600s, all ten of them though now whittled down to about six, would become part of automotive history.

George stayed on to the end still trying to capture the tail end of this elusive, half-breed stallion that he had nurtured since the original was born.

Today, George lives on the west coast of the USA dabbling in things non-auto related and doesn't even have a "sporty" car in his name. But he sure has a garage full of memories.

Karen (Clark) Bocsusis – Somewhere amid the dusty work space inside the Griffith Ford shop, George Clark had enlisted his fiancee' to assist him in building the protorype car and it only seemed the right thing to do.

George taught Karen to "tack weld" the pipes that he was assembling for the Griffith exhaust pipe headers and George would do the finishing work.

Just after the Griffith prototype was done, Karen and George got married and went to the Bahamas for their honeymoon. It was just about the time of the final visit of the Nassau Speed Weeks and the two newlyweds would end up spending their honeymoon working on the tech inspection crew and pitting for Carroll Shelby.

Ken Miles was driving the newly-introduced "Super Snake" and, as a gift, the Clark's honeymoon was underwritten by Carroll as a wedding present.

This partnership split up later on down the road but the two would meet once more when the Griffith crew was brought together in August, 2002 at the Saratoga Springs, New York, Griffith reunion.

Karen still follows the serious racing venues and keeps busy on the staff of a university back east.

Willie Seitz – Somewhere out in the far reaches of space float several pieces of space junk that have Willie's fingerprints affixed to their spheroid casings. More on that later, though.

What got him started in the wicked world of fast cars and faster crowds was simple; his dad owned a machine shop.

As a teenager, there would often be a big car to pick him up after school to shuttle him across town where the motor-magician, Bill Frick, would put Willie to work fabricating and machining parts to make Cadillac-powered Fords and Studebakers into weird and fast creations that would blow the doors off many unsuspecting rodders of the day.

Back to the the space junk. Willie's dad didn't own just any type of a machine shop, he owned a metal spinning operation that was flush with government contract work destined for the space effort.

Metal spinning consists of forming a piece of flat alloy material on a large lathe transforming it into a hemispherical shape, sort of like a stainless steel mixing bowl... sort of.

Many of these pieces would become the outer housings of the early satellites that are now the celestial flotsam known as space junk.

The Griffith Years

As someone who stood by Willie in the Griffith days watching him lighten pistons that were labeled "SuperLight" on the box, or recurve a Ford dual-point distributor on an old Sun machine, or explain the theory of why a set of small-diameter valves would be better than the super-sized ports, his sorcery was always amazing.

Sometimes I would just hang around to see what would happen next. He never was at a loss for mechanical innovations that would seem at first blush to be unworkable and foolish but when the smoke cleared, the cards would line up in a Royal Flush. It was because of an engine that Willie built that I was able to drive a street-driven '65, small-block Mustang to a quarter-mile trap time of 12.92 seconds and 111.76 mph in 1967.

Willie retired from the world of lathes and presses a few years back to farm some rocks and walking hamburgers in Pennsylvania. During the days of gathering information for this book, Willie's cast iron memory was the pillar that I relied on when some of the finer details were losing traction. He would sit down and almost verbatim, recite the litany of the times we spent together and the people we knew back then trying to make the darn little fiberglass car do things that Trevor Wilkinson never intended it to do.

Willie owns a white Griffith with blue strips down the middle and it's one that means a whole lot to him. When he first took a look at it on the lot in Florida he went over it with a fine-toothed comb. Turns out that it had weathered the ravages of time and still had all of the neat stuff that he had put on it in the early days of Griffith innovations. It was "Pure Willie!"

Len Bailey – Len started with the Griffith organization in May of 1964 as one of the factory assembly line workers and. One of his early jobs on the line, as he remembers, was to replace the "soft" bolts in the half shaft flanges with grade 5 or 6 bolts.

When production was at its peak, Len would take a car out for a "test drive" on the local streets about three or four times a week. It was necessary to check out most of the cars due to the frequent post-production problems that were encountered by the customer.

"A.J (Jack Griffith) would tell me when I took one out, 'If you lose, don't come back!' and there was usually a Corvette waiting for me to come out when I was road testing."

"It was a white-knuckle ride every time you took one out full throttle," Len added about his test drives. "You never knew which end was gonna go around the corner first, I mean, it was a rocket ship."

Growing up in West Hempstead, Len had attended the New York State University where he studied business administration. As with many of the youngsters of the day, Len got involved in sports car competition and he joined the Long Island Sports Car Association (LISCA) where he met Dick Monnich.

Len was driving a bright red 1952 Jaguar XK-120 fixed head coupe and often competed door-to-door with Denise McCluggage.

At one race in 1963, a sponsor signed aboard to help with the racing costs but the first race that he ran at Lime Rock, he lost a rear wheel and did not finish that day. His sponsor was Carl's Garage, a shop owned by Steve Levy and located on West 134th Street in New York City.

The following year, in 1964, Len went on to win the C-Production and D-Production championship with his Jaguar, and all this while he was driving and building Griffiths.

When Dick Monnich had decided that it was time to custom build a roadster Griffith car, Len was asked to build the "whale tail" spoiler on the rear deck, not dissimilar to the Porsche Targa and later models.

"I remember when I brought Mark (Donohue) to the back room to show him his 'Sebring' car," Len recalled. "The skin was so thin you could read a newspaper through it."

"…That car never turned a wheel in anger" according to Len.

Research shows that it was reportedly sold, along with the repainted "plaid" car, to a Michigan Ford dealer, named Gene Balmes. After reskinning the roadster and strengthening the chassis, Gene campaigned it and the repainted "plaid" car in regional sports car competition both as a "prototype" Griffiths. So far neither car has surfaced but the search goes on, already with some solid leads.

Though Len stayed on through the transition to the Series 400 car, he had left prior to the 600 going into full production. Len said that when Bob Cumberford, one of the designers of the last model Griffith, began working on the new series car, "…he spent weeks at the factory; we worked together three or four weeks… making a clay [mock-up] of the car. We used a donor chassis from a destroyed TVR car as the platform and to make the body shape we were using blocks of styrofoam and sliced them down to form the body."

Just before Len was left the factory, he did remember the first Series 600 car arriving, a yellow one, that was then fitted with the Ford engine. But when the Ford deal went south, the 289 was yanked and the MoPar 273 cubic inch engine was installed.

Len went on to other pursuits after the Griffith experience and eventually started up a tour bus company driving slower and less maneuverable vehicles than the Griffiths around the highways of America.

Since selling the company a few yers ago Len semi-retired. For a daily driver he has a Jaguar sedan and still enjoys following good, competitive auto racing. He is one of the few original Griffith "players" who still resides on Long Island.

Bob Cumberford – For a designer to be called on to bring a car into the world at the hands of another's purse strings is probably the things that dreams are made of. Bob Cumberford had been working with General Motors in the design department and at other projects of personal interest… and then the call came in.

Jack Griffith wanted a new GT version of his new car and would look towards a designer who could deliver the crisp translation of the idea. Bob Cumberford teamed up with John Crostwaithe to put the plan on paper, or did they?

Lurking in the woodpile was an Alfa Romeo designer named Franco Scaglione who claimed that the idea was his and it just might have been.

Somewhere along the way the two might have worked together and a bit of cross-talk in lines on the paper could have occurred but, eventually, the objection was lost somewhere in the dust.

With several ideas on the drawing pad the final design came in about nine months late for Jack Griffith but he had it in hand… finally, and Frank Reisner at Intermeccanica in Turin, Italy was given the challenge to translate the ideas into a set of bucks and to put the body on a set of wheels.

Cumberford did his job and he did it well. What he designed would become a bellwether of design ideas that would be partially repeated in other marques, truly a mark of design genius. Sadly, it took a dock strike to help to douse the flame.

Dave Schineller – Perched up on his position in the shop out back at Griffith Ford, Dave assumed the job of service manager for the dealership. An easy going gentle man, Dave wouldn't let too much get in his way for unnecessary aggravation. He could have probably gotten the job as the poster boy for service managers and it showed.

Just behind his work station in one of the two service buildings at the Ford dealership Jack had Roger Teck set up the work area for the Griffith Sprint project and then when George Clark was assigned the task of both the Sprint and the Griffith prototype, they became close friends.

The Griffith Years

In October of '64 when this writer spun a bearing in his (Griffith Ford-bought) HiPo Mustang just about a month out of the box and was towed in on the business end of Gus Redlinger's tow truck, Dave noticed (oops!) that there was a pair of four-barrel carburetors atop the engine where there used to be just one.

Realizing that Ford was doing all in its power to make the new high performance program to succeed, Dave quickly had the dual quads removed, hidden and a stock, single quad set-up put in its place for the district representative to inspect. It was OK... the engine was replaced under the meager 3,000 mile/3 month drive line warranty. That was Dave!

Dave had started working in the Ford network at Levittown Ford as a prep man in the shop remaining there from 1954 through 1960 when he was hired at White-Griffith Motors. This was just about the time that Lou Benny left his partnership with Jack Griffith.

After staying there through all of the dealership name changes that followed Griffith, including Bob-Ken Ford (owned by Bob Wallace and Ken Gilkes), McDaniel Ford and Hicksville Ford, Dave retired from the Ford family in 1988.

John Fisher – Working just down the row of work bays at Griffith Ford was an amiable and outspoken mechanic who was never at a loss for good conversation or a strong opinion.

John was the one person who made probably the most profound statement about the Griffith. When queried about the car he said, "...the whole problem with the Griffith was that the car was never evaluated."

That was not the first time that John made a profound statement. On September 23, 1964, when my brand new High Performance Mustang was delivered, I did what I had to do. I went to the Shell gas station down the street to fill the tank with high test gasoline.

Hell, at 32.9 cents a gallon, it was the least I could do and, besides, Jack Griffith's sales crew didn't leave but enough gasoline in the fuel tank to get me out of the showroom and down the street.

In that first 2 miles of my car ownership, I noticed that there was an intermittent miss in the engine compartment, so I drove right back and into the shop. As Dave Schineller heard my tale of woe, he told me to pull it into a work bay for a check up.

With the solid lifters noisily making their rounds on the cam in this 271 horsepower car, the first of its kind to be delivered from the dealership, just about the entire shop-full of mechanics were hovering about the engine bay looking at the screens of the electronic scopes that were hooked up to the engine, but no one could figure it out.

In the next bay, John Fisher was cleaning up at the end of the day and was pushing the broom around his work area. In a lull of the conversations that were going on under my hood, John stopped them all in their tracks with one sentence.

"It sounds like a loose condenser."

John's observation was noted. They shut the engine down and one of the gathered techs pulled the distributor cap and, sure enough, the condenser was loose. A quick draw on the duty screwdriver solved the problem and I was on my way. That's all! That's John!

Bobby Brown, Jr. – The son of a Chevrolet dealer whose silver spoon was the Corvette with which he would assault the drag strips and "traffic-light Grands Prix" would cave to an assignation with Jack Griffith's Ford-powered Cobra.

As someone who would luckily have some of the neatest friends of the time, like Willie Seitz, George Clark and Roger Teck, Bobby would go on to make his name in racing and trying his best to break the rolling stock in his barn.

Later on he'd have his fun piloting some very fast Trans-Am Camaros with Willie Seitz-tuned and built engines. Most people weren't privy to some of Bobby's tricks, but when Willie did the engine up right, the competition didn't know what hit them. I think that it was the gray paint on the engine… I think.

Joe Quinn – The sales manager at Griffith Ford who lured me into the show room there in Hicksville with an offer that I couldn't resist. I bought the car and the car owned me after that.

Joe has stayed in the trade over the years, the most recent contact with him was in the midst of a car wholesale deal he was cutting. I know that Joe will sell a car to St. Peter himself!

Pete Elardo – One of the salesmen at Griffith Ford who was a quiet man, but had a salesman's mustache. You've seen them. Clark Gable had one, David Niven had one… and Pete had one.

Not of any interest to the Griffith movement, but I ended working with Joe for about four months back in '86 in another Ford dealership, just before he made his last payment. God Bless ya, Pete.

Ralph Olesen – Working as a part time starter and mechanic at Griffith Motorcar, Inc., Ralph was the one who, among others, manned the big sledge hammer prepping the TVR chassis for the engine installation.

Ralph went on to become an engineer who learned how to do it right, without the big hammer.

Peter Dodge – One of the first workers hired at Griffith along with Joey DeTore. Peter was remembered by a couple of those interviewed but we were unable to locate him.

Mike Martorano – Mike's time at Griffith was recollected by one of the other factory workers but was unable to provide us with the correct spelling of his last name nor provide any leads as to his whereabouts.

Joey Detore – "Hey, Mikey!" Joey would call to me when he wanted to make a point or tell me something. I first met Joey in October, 1964 when he was driving his "low performance" 'Stang and I was in my HiPo "K" model. There was something that made me want to stay around. Maybe it was because of his arrogance towards my belief of what I thought was "the most powerful Mustang around." He then proceeded to "whup my butt" with his car. What I didn't know at the time was that the engine in his car was out of Willie Seitz's shop.

He was a true character who knew how to get attention. Hanging out at his "post-Griffith" gas station, I was invited to go with him to make a bank deposit. His "car du jour" was a modified and Corvair-powered Meyers Manx dune buggy so we settled in for a short drive down the street.

At the drive-in window he pulled up to see who was on duty, backed up about fifty feet, dropped it into first and proceeded to do a nerf bar-scraping wheelstand through the porte' cochere, dropped the front wheels back down on the ground, backed up to the window, and just said "Hi!"

This was also the impatient and fledgeling student pilot who assembled a Piper Cub in the gas station on Veterans Memorial Highway in his spare time. When it came time to tow the aircraft down to MacArthur airport, he instead opted to attach the wings to the fuselage outside on the tarmac at the gas station, had some friends stop traffic, taxied out onto the highway and took off.

The last time I saw Joey, he was on TV playing the role of a throttle man on one of those multi-thousand horsepower, triple-engined off-shore racing boats… and that was after the brain surgery which left him with a steel plate implanted in his skull.

In the brief time that Joey spent on this earth, shortened by Lou Gehrig's disease, he had filled with just about two lifetimes.

Jim Ketcher – As a young and impressionable car-guy, Jim was told by his dad of a new car manufacturer in Syosset that he had heard was hiring and might be worth checking into. Jim's dad was a hardware salesman who had stopped off at Eileen Drive and had seen the operation.

Jim had been working at Foreign Car Corporation, an import car dealer in Bay Shore on Long Island and dropped in to the Syosset plant to be interviewed by Dick Triano in July of '64.

"I got the job in late summer or early fall that year," Jim recalled. "I became part of the team working first to remove the leaky gasoline tanks and then to help pick up the car bodies as they arrived at the port in New York Harbor. Eventually I was assigned to finish-prep the cars for delivery."

As was noted earlier, Jim had probably been the first driver of a good number of all the new Griffiths as they came off the line. His observations and driving impressions were classic "nouveau driver." As a relatively young newcomer to the trade, his take on this potent little car were more subjective rather than from being spoken by a biased and seasoned driver.

At one point during his time at Griffith, Jim was assigned to prep the prototype car for the Chicago Auto Show and when Dick Monnich returned from the show, Jim was congratulated for his detail in preparing the car for the trip.

When the "great purge" had to be carried out by the shop manager, Dick Triano, Jim was one of those released and his time at Griffith was history.

Life after Griffith took Jim to continue his education and he eventually went on to take a position as an engineer at a helicopter and aviation manufacturer in Connecticut.

Bob Bergen – Just a short note about the guy who had the acorns to take on the job of painting the "plaid" Griffith for the Car show in New York. There were two things that Bob said that he would never do again in his life at his Pioneer Auto Body shop.

First was that he would never again restore a Plymouth Barracuda and the other was that he would never paint a plaid car.

Gerry Sagerman – A full blooded sports car nut, Gerry was one of the "bookends" of the Griffith era. Long before the Cobra was part of America's vernacular, he had raced with Mark Donohue at Sebring.

He was a constant part of the formative times of sports car racing here in the Colonies and lived to see it come full turn. When drivers were the mechanics and vice-versa, when sponsorship consisted of a free tank of traveling gas and maybe a few quarts of oil, when car owners knew more about the inner workings of the car than the engineers who designed the mechanicals of the beast, Gerry had his fun in the driver's seat.

When Dick Monnich was unseated as the import maven of the TVR, Gerry took on the job and became its most loyal promoter. He not only drove the cars on the track just about every weekend, Gerry also made sure that the TVR group was well represented on this side of the pond.

Gerry became part of the legacy of the Griffith years. His foresight in the future of the marriage between the little TVR and the Ford V-8 power would help him to convince Martin Lilly to continue the story.

The Griffith Years

Stephen Wilder – When Jack Griffith was putting the team together he needed a public relations firm that could translate his message to the masses who would become the buyers and fans. He chose the Joe Lane agency to do the bidding.

One of the writers on board was Steve Wilder, a nonchalant and affable fellow who had a knack of being able to put the right words in the right places.

He had worked on the Griffith account helping to promote the marque and the idea. It served as a springboard to getting to know the inner working of being a car company president.

An engineer trained at M.I.T. where he concentrated on vehicle stability and control, put his knowledge and experience to a practical application as a racing driver, test driver, technical writer and road tester for Car and Driver magazine.

Since his college days, Wilder had raced cars throughout the States and in Europe having fun and living the good life. In the writing arena, Wilder was well known for his numerous articles, mostly technical, regarding automobiles and racing and had been published, in addition to C&D, within the pages of Hot Rod magazine, Automobile Quarterly, Road and Track, Autoweek and Car Life, all well known motorsports lifestyle magazines.

When the Griffith project went sour Steve was waiting in the wings and along with Gerry Sagerman and Bob Cumberford, the threesome tried to resurrect the Intermeccanica body from the ashes.

The partnership would not last too long and Steve found himself awash in car bodies and the new owner of a car company. He contacted the Holman-Moody team in Charlotte, North Carolina to help with prolonging the life of the design.

H-M put a young fabricator named Larry Jenkins at the head of the department and they named the car "Omega." In the Greek alphabet, the letter "omega" is "the end." Strange, wot?

The Plymouth engines were "out" and Ford was back under the hood. The Holman-Moody team did their magic to wring out the last bit of uncivilized power from the Ford small block.

Steve had a briefcase full of his own money to give wings to the car but as the needs of selling the car grew, the briefcase got smaller and smaller. He learned how a person could make a small fortune building cars, and that was to start out with a large fortune.

Thirty cars later the Omega car company was history and Steve learned one very expensive lesson… don't ever try to become the president of a car company again.

Steve would go on in other directions, mostly writing and public relations but he would never get to do anything as magnificent as owning a car company.

Don Johnson – To be successful, a company needs a talented and knowledgable treasurer and comptroller to keep watch over the purse strings as it grows and Jack had one person in mind. He picked his brother-in-law, Don Johnson, with some experience in the aerospace field, who stepped up to the plate and took over the financial reins.

A quiet member of the work force, Don would keep track of the cash flow but didn't venture too often into the bowels of the work shop out back in the factory. His job was to keep the company on the straight and narrow but had his hands full once the dock strike took its toll.

Donald F. Millager – Originally hired as sales manager at Griffith. He was the car salesman who sold Jack his first sports car in 1948, an MG-TC, the 46th of its kind to be imported into the U.S. following WWII.

Larry Jenkins – When Holman-Moody took over the job of exploiting the future of the Series 600 Intermeccanica body a young engineer and fabricator was chosen to head up the project. Larry Jenkins worked with Steve Wilder to attempt to make the silk purse out of the sow's ear.

The Griffith Years

The first thing that was done was to heave out the Plymouth engine and replace it with its original power, the venerable and much lighter Ford 289. Then, as their investigation and evaluation (there's that word again!) continued, the problems that were encountered numbered somewhere near 300.

Larry recalls that one handling problem was that on hard acceleration from a start, the steering wheel required a sixty-degree rotation to keep the car in a straight line. To cut to the root of the puzzle, he and Steve had to poke out a hole in the body panel just atop the differential and under the hard acceleration, Larry would be perched inside the rear shelf area peering down into the hole to watch what was happening that might cause this geometric anomoly. It worked; they found the problem.

Larry went on to turn his knowledge of automotive engineering and now conducts business maintaining high-end cars for their particular owners just about a par five from the old Holman-Moody plant near Douglas International Airport in Charlotte, North Carolina.

The Griffith Years

ten

Car 54
Where Are You?

...with respectful apologies to Toody and Muldoon.

"The Griffith is not just a car... it is a passion!"
Robert Goldschmidt

Griffith chassis # 200-5-054 was meant to be, as all cars of the marque were predisposed, a bold motoring statement and a rolling example of a totally dramatic presentation.

photo courtesy of Bob Goldschmidt

Car "54" awaiting its fate

The Griffith Years

Easter Sunday, 1983, a warm and sunny day in Pennsylvania, promised to be a combination of a family homecoming and a gathering at the Goldschmidt home. Bob Goldschmidt's twin-brother, Paul, would be traveling up from Virginia and Bob's girlfriend, Michelle was stopping by for the day.

"The misfit among misfits, Dave [Livingstone], and his Series 200 Griffith, an explosive combination trying to tempt destiny, was there," according to Bob. "A match made in hell!"

The holiday spirit was gathering momentum as the crowd enjoyed taking photos of the cute little car outside at the curb.

"I asked Dave to drive it so I could get a picture of the Griffith in motion," Bob said, "and he was more than happy to oblige my request."

Just after arriving Dave had learned that Paul had never tasted of the thrill of riding in such a fast car and asked if he wanted to come along for the photo shoot. But Paul was well aware of Dave's driving record as well as his reputation of piloting in the foolish little fiberglass "toy" so he wasn't too quick to jump at the chance.

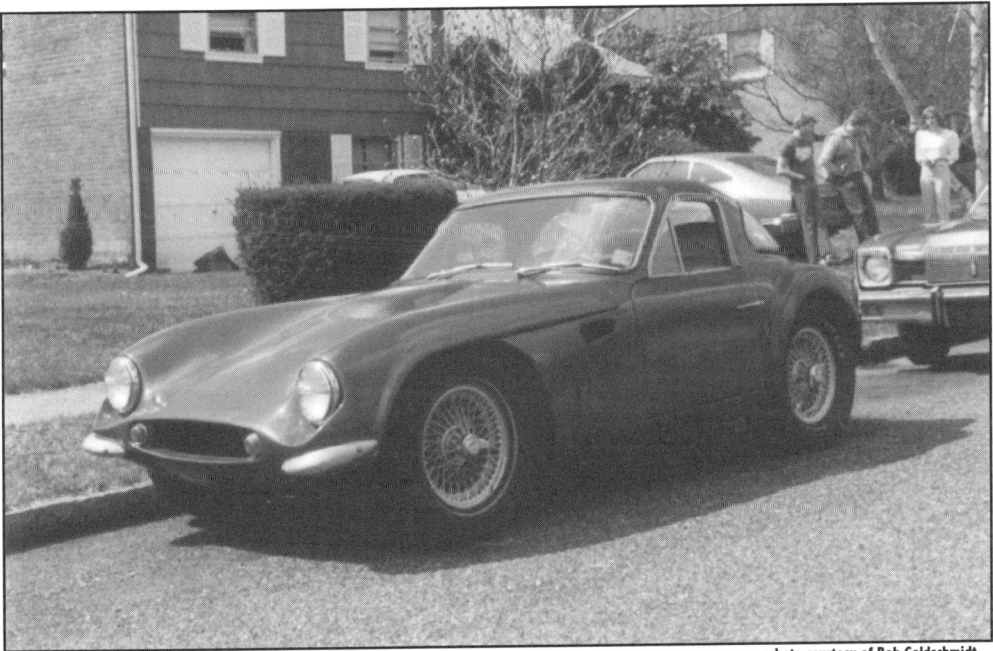

photo courtesy of Bob Goldschmidt

The crowd gathers for the photo shoot

"Seeing my brother's concern, I spoke up confidently… that nothing could happen just down the road and back; that Dave wouldn't do anything stupid," Bob added. "Then Michelle mentioned that even she had gone for a ride and thought it had been fun!"

The plot thickened for them all. Father Fate was rubbing his hands gleefully.

Paul approached the car reluctantly, looking back wondering whether he should trust all of those who had known him and cared for his safety, but he continued, slowly.

He climbed into the car looking over his shoulder at us as if he were a prisoner being strapped into the deadly grasp of an electric chair. The joy of the crowd was soon drowned out by the roar of a powerful 289 HiPo being cranked to life, clearing its throat seeking out yet another victim.

Dave edged the car away from the curb and, surprisingly, not-too-quickly disappeared over the hill preparing to turn around for the show. Since the car was out of sight, the crowd had only the sound of the car to rely on for cues to get the cameras ready.

With their ears peeled they all heard the car come to a stop and then listened to the revs of the engine huffing its way through a three point turn getting into position for a pass by the house.

"The Griffith suddenly changed to a full throttle blast of thunder," Bob recalled. "Dave meant business!"

The pure sound of power put smiles on the faces of just about everyone standing on the front lawn, all but some of the neighbors who had heard the cacophonous noises that the Grif was emitting, but what the heck, it was a holiday, and holidays are for fun.

As quickly as our smiles appeared, they suddenly disappeared. The full throttle noise of the car accelerating in first was shattered by the sound of screeching tires and the explosion of steel, aluminum and fiberglass. Then… complete silence; just too quiet.

"I knew something happened and it wasn't good," Bob remembered of that day. "I watched almost every neighbor run out of their homes towards the sound of the accident."

When the bulk of the neighborhood crowd descended on the scene the sight only said that someone was hurt and hurt bad. There were pieces of car and everything all over the place. The situation looked dim for both riders.

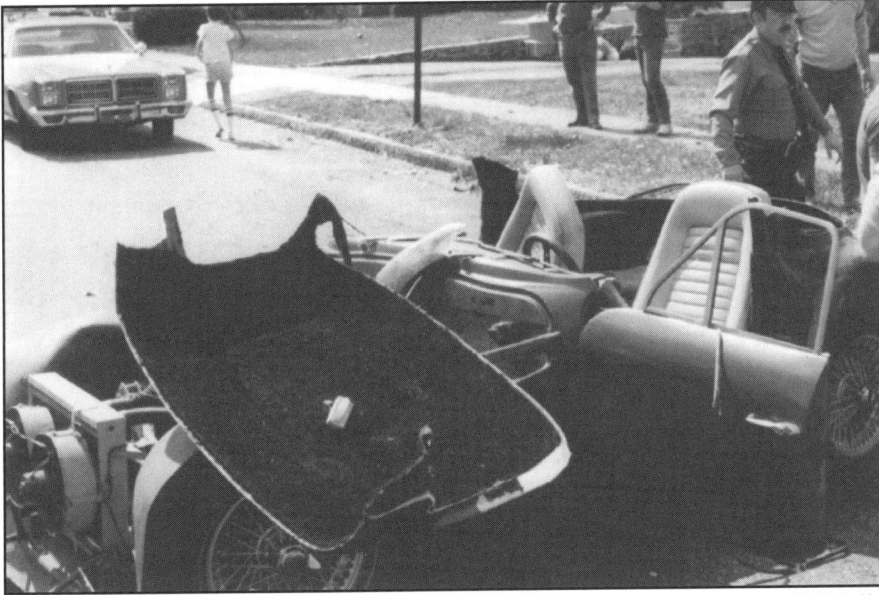

photo courtesy of Bob Goldschmidt

Car "54" just moments after the crash

"Injuries were surprisingly minimal," said Bob. "Dave broke his nose, but was basically intact, except for his brain, but that was never right to begin with."

Paul ended up with minor cuts and bruises, quite surprising for the damage that was visited upon the car. He actually ended up being thrown from the car and landing about twenty feet away landing on his rump still holding the passenger door which was now lying next to him on the ground.

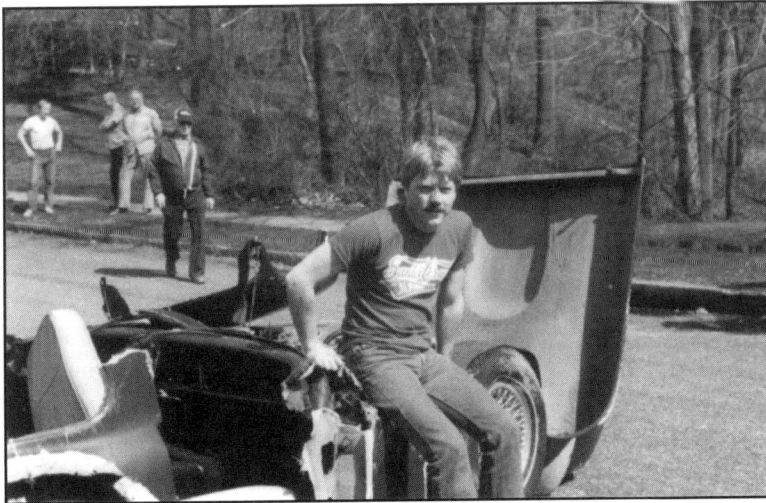

photo courtesy of Bob Goldschmidt

Dave Livingstone's finest moment
Note: Neighbor walking toward car in background is about to chew out Dave for his driving skills.

The Griffith Years

Bob had just about reached the site of the destruction when Paul, looking around at what had just happened and what led up to the ride, stood up picking up the door by whatever was left of it and threw it at Dave, muttering something about where he could store it.

In the aftermath of what caused the totally destructive events leading up to the crash Bob reckoned that, with the sound that the engine had been making just before the silence, a power shift into second gear had done just what the early drivers of the little car had experienced… which end goes first when the wheels lose traction?

Slow motion descriptions by many of the local "traffic accident experts" revealed many "guess-timates" most indicating that when the car started to lose forward traction it skidded sideways towards the curb. As it side-slid into the concrete curbing the car went airborne, flipping over at least once as it was looking for a safe place to land.

"I suppose it's only fair to give Dave the benefit of the doubt as to the cause [of the accident]," according to Bob. "In the end it was only a matter of fate."

photo courtesy of Bob Goldschmidt

Car "54" awaiting a thorough top-to-bottom restoration.

"Somehow my brother was ejected out of the door," Bob recalled. "He distinctly remembers the sensation of mid-air flight."

The car ended on what was left of its wheels across the middle of the road awaiting the wail of the local police sirens.

Bob said that he eventually bought the remnants of car number 054, donating the engine to a Shelby GT-350 that he was restoring and then selling the remains of the Griffith.

The old body is still now languishing in a garage somewhere waiting for its owner to gather up enough parts and time so that the old beast can be brought back to life and again enjoy the "exciting life" of high performance motoring.

Or maybe it'll just become someone's trophy, the prize that only those who have experienced the thrill and unpredictability of a Griffith can lay claim to.

The Griffith Years

eleven

The Legacy

"..What's past is prologue"
William Shakespeare

When the Series 600 Intermeccanica-built, Cumberford-designed car met its premature end, the car refused to lay down and die. Some of the caretakers of the marque from within and without were ready to try to keep the body design alive.

PR and automotive writer Steve Wilder, all-around car guy Gerry Sagerman and car designer Bob Cumberford, were all ready to see if the body would be able withstand another assault on the motoring public by forming a company incongruously named "Suspension International Corporation" with home offices listed at 11 Middle Drive in the toney neighborhood of Manhasset, Long Island, New York.

This company would later use the Holman-Moody address in Charlotte, North Carolina on their correspondence.

Early on, the Reisner-based design would be called into check by someone who claimed the design rights. Franco Scaglione worked with Reisner on the early Buick-powered sports coupe named the Apollo. According to Scaglione he had designed the follow-up car that would eventually become the "GOTI" (Griffith-Omega-Torino-Italia) car.

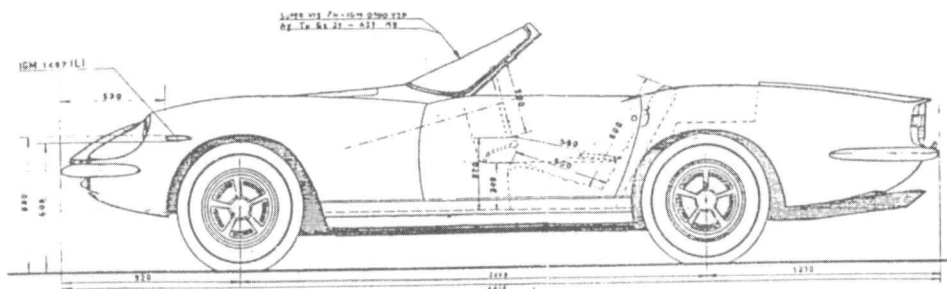

Design print of Intermeccanica Italia Roadster

Prior to the Italia, Torino, Omega or Griffith name plates were affixed to the body panels, Reisner went through several business partners and names carrying the design in his briefcase. The questions is probably still being argued about in the finest pubs of the States and in Europe. When the jury comes in, we'll probably be the last to know.

It was here that the collaboration with Holman-Moody for the project was steeled but soon the partnership would fall apart with Steve holding the last of the pieces. With a car that would present so many design problems, the future was cast in stone when Larry Jenkins and Wilder would try their best to come up with a solution to what could have become Ford's answer to the ever-popular Chevrolet Corvette.

With H-M so deeply embedded with Ford in the competition endeavors and their relationship to Carroll Shelby's research on the GT-40, and had the car been given a better genetic helix in Italy, it could have risen from the ashes a winner.

When all thirty or thirty-three cars were sold and the stock depleted, Omega took to its name, in Greek, "the end" and folded. Frank Reisner was getting exhausted watching his creation looking more like a traveling salesman going from door-to-door trying to find a buyer.

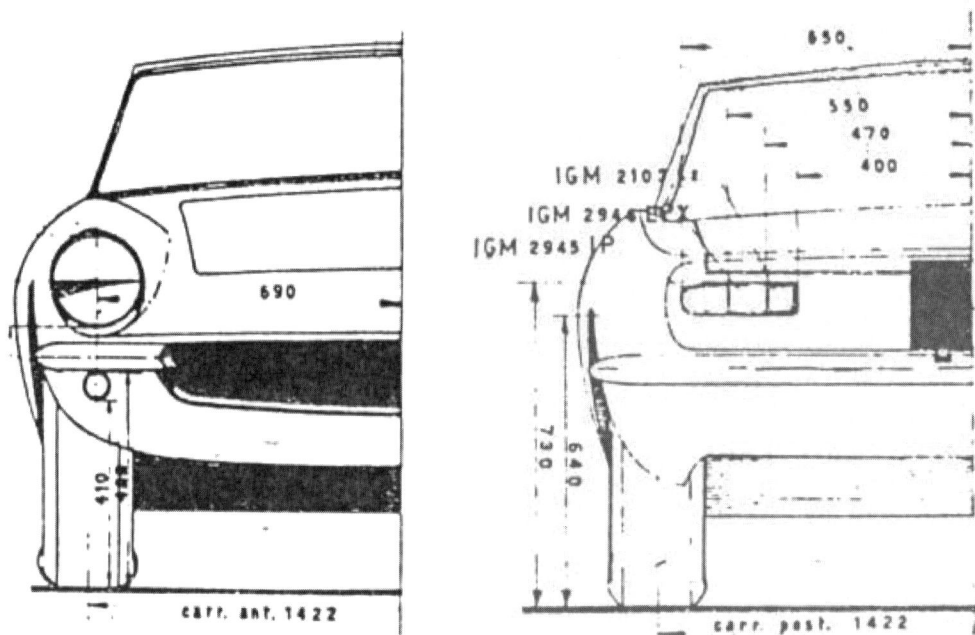

Drawings by Cumberford/Intermeccanica – courtesy of Jack Griffith collection

Engineering and Design renderings of the Intermeccanica car

A new name was now put on the fender and hood. The Torino was born but Ford objected due to the fact that they owned the name plate and that idea was short-lived.

Drawings by Cumberford/Intermeccanica – courtesy of Jack Griffith collection

Rendering of proposed Griffith design

140

Reisner approached Jack Griffith again to see if he could help in resurrecting the project car that was now well into and past its second adoptive name and looking at the world through the window of the orphanage once again.

The car took on another name… the car was rechristened the Italia this time being assembled at the Turin offices of Intermeccanica. Sounds an awful lot like Yogi Berra was writing the script for this one. An old friend of Jack's took on the stateside distributorship for the newly-badged car. Genser-Foreman, a New Jersey dealership known for its handling of imported sports cars, asked Jack to come aboard to handle the account.

As soon as Genser-Foreman signed on as reps of the newly-named old timer and agreed to handle the distribution of the car, it was reported that they got a letter from Resiner saying that he didn't need Jack anymore.

Whoa! Genser-Foreman had been dealing with Jack Griffith for a few more years than the Italian connection had and that request didn't hold too well with them. Jack was a good connection here in the states and held the respect with many of the dealers with whom he had been working both as a Ford dealer and as a manufacturer.

Genser-Foreman dropped Frank Reisner like the proverbial hot potato and the two split. The bell rang marking an end to Round Four. Once again Reisner was back to square one.

According to loosely kept records there were reportedly a total of between 450 and 500 copies of the design built under the four trade names. The later Italias were still powered by Ford engines but were upgraded to the 351 cubic inch Windsor powerplants rated from 285 and 300 horsepower. Also according to Matthew Stone as reported in Super Ford magazine, since many of the Italia cars were custom built for the owners, a floor-shifted automatic and Ford four-speed manual transmissions were available options.

The Griffith Years

Nearing the end of its life, a truly interesting, variant design based on this car was produced in the form of a stunning and wild-looking high-performance station wagon named the Murena. This truly Euro-design was powered with the new Ford 429 cid block under the bonnet. In the end count, there were only ten of these built.

After the Series 600 and it clones were history Jack Griffith didn't stop creating. This human dynamo tilted on yet another windmill in the automotive market. Let's see where we can go from here. He developed the Dingbat. This was a little 850 cc-powered dune buggy-type that was marketed, or attempted to be marketed, from a firm named Chassis Unlimited, Inc. located in Fort Lee, New Jersey. The sales brochure listed Jack Griffith as President.

courtesy Jack Griffith collection

Dingbat 850 logo

After moving to Fort Lauderdale, Florida in 1974, Jack came out of retirement and decided to make a go of it again. With an idea based on the Toyota Celica body that was produced from 1979 through '84 Jack decided to go "topless." Well, not really Jack, but the car was treated to a little cosmetic surgery in the form of a model called the "Sunchaser."

What Jack did was to lop off the roof of the car and had his crew make it into a Targa-topped type of convertible, perfect for the Sunshine State.

The Griffith Years

After starting the company in southern Florida near his home with yet another plant in Santa Ana, California, he moved to a location that was deserted by Ford a few years back, a plant called Talleyrand near his new home in Jacksonville.

From the Celica body conversion, Jack moved on to developing a true convertible conversion based on the Toyota Corolla which was dubbed The Griffith Limited. All in all, about 6,000 drop-tops were built with production rates never exceeding 200 units a month. Jack said that he wanted to produce about 300 per month and the Southeast Toyota dealers wanted 400.

Photos courtesy Motor Trend Magazine

The Griffith Toyota Sunchaser conversion

During the production time line of these cars, a voice from the past was raised with a comment on the current convertible boomlet that a few, including Griffith, were enjoying. Tony Baumgartner, Intermeccanica president, worried that too many shoddy shops turning out shoddy cars will eventually spoil it for the entire mini-industry. "It's going to die in four years," he warned.

At the time, **Intermeccanica Automobili**, now located in Fountain Valley, California, was producing Ford Mustang convertible conversions, all of this activity following Detroit's decision to phase out all drop-heads in 1976. Peter Fonda ordered the last Cadillac Eldorado rag-top and someone penned a novel called **"The Last Convertible."** Jack was riding the wave.

"Everybody in this business is a big kid," Baumgartner added, "and fortunately there are an awful lot of people in the United states just like us."

The Griffith Years

At one time he drove a drop-top Toyota to the new Genser-Foreman showroom in New York City and parked it out front on the corner of Broadway and 56th Street. Still truly a showman, Jack said that it drew a huge crowd and literally stopped traffic.

Besides the Toyota variant, Jack also produced Targa versions of AMC's Javelin and Concord as well as a special truck model and the Datsun 280Z drop-top before he sold out the company.

That wasn't the end, though. As you might remember in the beginning of the book, it was mentioned that Jack just couldn't stand still. He decided to go into the boat business.

The Griffith convertible conversion of a Datsun 280-Z

With his experience in boating, Jack tried to develop a boat tht didn't have a propeller. Now quite a common sight on the waterways of the world, mostly in personal watercraft, Jack dabbled in jet-drive units. What was dubbed as "the boat that didn't need water" by one journalist, became the next **"project du jour"** for Jack. Jack retired in 1985… I think!

As Jack's constant presence in the automotive industry began to ebb, his name did not. After the weakened TVR corporate structure nearly doomed the marque to the withered pages of the history books, and following several ownership changes, it rebounded to become what is now one of the foremost high performance automobile manufacturers in the U.K.

Not only are they producing the later versions of cars dreamed up by Trevor Wilkinson more than a half-century ago, following the collapse of the Griffith marque in 1967 they also started to produce the V-8 powered TVR Tuscan following a few remnantal versions of the Griffith, a long wheelbase version of the car, as well as a few variants of what Jack Griffith had begun.

In 1982 Peter Wheeler, the current owner of the company, took over control of TVR from Martin Lilley and Stewart Halstead became managing director. A year later the company tried their hand once more with the V-8 and dropped a Rover (Buick design) 3.5 liter into the "wedge-bodied" Tasmin body and the TVR 350i was born.

The following year they redesigned the wedge body rounding the fenders a bit and launched the 390SE powered by a 275 bhp engine, TVR's Supercar. The fever built!

During the next few years several design innovations were incorporated including a SEAC model, SEAC standing for Special Equipment Aramid Composite, with some of the body being constructed with a near-Kevlar construction. Bulletproof cars were here to stay.

Over the next four years Peter Wheeler bought out the Halstead partnership and proceeded to introduce several models of varying high performance vehicles that could easily dust whatever the competition could bring and he also launched a Tuscan Challenge cars for competition.

1990 saw the introduction of an idea that would again bring the Griffith name back into the automotive arena. Wheeler introduced a prototype car named the Griffith and set the design and engineering staff to work on a neat idea.

TVR Griffith Drop Head

TVR ran with the project and in 1992 the first "second generation" Griffith was delivered, generating an enormous demand with its aerodynamic styling and rounded fenders. This exercise transmuted into fitting a new AJP V-8 powered TVR model named the Cerbera. This engine was actually used for the first time in competition in the Tuscan Challenge cars but was not introduced to the public until installed in the Cerbera. 2001 was the last year that the Griffith name was used on a TVR bodied car.

Over the years, from 1963 when George Clark built the first Griffith prototype car on Route 106/107 in Hicksville, New York until 2001, thirty years later, the quiet legend of Jack Griffith has lived in the active annals of automotive history. The name will not die so long as there are drivers who want to experience the joy of having an extremely lightweight car with an overpowered and wild engine under the hood to take them to places that the regulated motorcars of today cannot or will not.

In 1992 when Jack Griffith was first interviewed for this book he was asked if he would do it all over again. His reply was cautious yet prophetic.

"I don't know how much further we could have gone because [government] regulations got tougher. People came to me and asked me to do it again but with the regulations today it would be impossible."

The Griffith Years

If you take the time to sit down with Jack anytime and start him talking about his experiences over the years, you'll see the unquenchable smile and the gleam in his eye saying without uttering a word, "Yes, I'd do it again!"

The Griffith Years

photo courtesy of Chris McArdle

Series 200-5-149

The Griffith Years

Price (as shown): $3995.00
F.O.B. Syosset, New York

Bonnie..
Brawny..
Thrifty too...
presenting
the Grrrrreat GRIFFITH Series 200

Additional reading & hyperlinks

The Unfair Advantage   by Mark Donohue (Bentley Publishers)
TVRs   (multi-volumes) by Graham Robson (Motor Racing Publications, Ltd.)
TVR: Success Against the Odds   by Peter J. Filby (Wilton House Gentry)
TVR The Complete Story   by John Tipler (Crowood PR)
TVR Griffith and Chimaera   by Steve Heath
TVR   by John Tipler
TVR Performance Portfolio 1995-2000   by R.M. Clarke
TVR (Sutton's Photographic History of Transport)   by John Tipler
TVR Road Test Book   by R.M. Clarke
----

www.griffithclub.com

http://members.cts.com/sd/j/jnlrauh/index.html

http://www.tvrcc.com/

http://cognac.lu.se/tvr/links-tvr.html

http://www.tvr-eng.co.uk/tvr.htm

http://www.tvr.co.uk/

www.gspovey.demon.co.uk/garage/tvr/

www.tvrbooks.co.uk/

www.hemmings.com

www.motorlibrary.com/mak/tvr.htm

www.motolit.com/cars-make-tvr.html

http://www.quicklink.ms/tvr.html

www.amazon./com

http://www.barnesandnoble.com/

http://www.pistonheads.com/tvr/griffith/

http://www.bordersstores.com/index.jsp

The Griffith Years